CONVERSATIONAL
SPANISH

THE LIVING LANGUAGE™ SERIES
BASIC COURSES ON CASSETTE
   *Spanish
   *French
   *German
   *Italian
   *Japanese
   *Portuguese (Continental)
   Portuguese (South American)
   Advanced Spanish
   Advanced French
   Children's Spanish
   Children's French
   Russian
   Hebrew
   English for Native Spanish Speakers
   English for Native French Speakers
   English for Native Italian Speakers
   English for Native German Speakers
   English for Native Chinese Speakers

*Also available on Compact Disc

LIVING LANGUAGE PLUS®
   Spanish
   French
   German
   Italian

LIVING LANGUAGE TRAVELTALK™
   Spanish
   French
   German
   Italian
   Russian

CONVERSATIONAL
SPANISH

A COMPLETE COURSE
IN EVERYDAY SPANISH

By Ralph Weiman

EDUCATIONAL DIRECTOR LIVING LANGUAGE
COURSES. FORMERLY CHIEF OF LANGUAGE
SECTION, U.S. WAR DEPARTMENT

AND

O.A. Succar

HEAD OF SPANISH DEPARTMENT
LIVING LANGUAGE COURSES

SPECIALLY PREPARED FOR USE WITH
THE LIVING LANGUAGE COURSE IN SPANISH

Crown Publishers, Inc., New York

This work was previously published under the title *Conversation Manual Spanish*.

Copyright © 1946, 1955, 1968, 1974, 1983, 1985 by Crown Publishers, Inc.

THE LIVING LANGUAGE COURSE is a registered trademark, and CROWN, and LIVING LANGAGE and colophon are trademarks of Crown Publishers, Inc., 201 East 50th Street, New York, N.Y. 10022.

Library of Congress Catalog Card Number: 55-12164

ISBN 0-517-55787-8

1985 Updated Edition

Manufactured in the United States of America

27   26   25   24

TABLE OF CONTENTS

INTRODUCTION to the COMPLETE LIVING LANGUAGE COURSE®

The Living Language Course® uses the natural method of language-learning. You learn Spanish the way you learned English—by hearing the language and repeating what you heard. You didn't begin by studying grammar; you first learned how to say things, how words are arranged, and only when you knew the language pretty well did you begin to study grammar. This course teaches you Spanish in the same way. Hear it, say it, absorb it through use and repetition. The only difference is that in this course the basic elements of the language have been carefully selected and condensed into 40 short lessons. When you have finished these lessons, you will have a good working knowledge of the language. If you apply yourself, you can master this course and learn to speak basic Spanish in a few weeks.

While *Living Language™ Conversational Spanish* is designed for use with the complete Living Language Course®, this book may be used without the cassettes. The first 5 lessons cover Spanish pronunciation, laying the foundation for learning the vocabulary, phrases, and grammar that are explained in the later chapters.

All the material is presented in order of importance. When you reach page 150, you will have already learned 300 of the most frequently used sentences and will be able to make yourself understood on many important topics. By the time you have finished this course, you will have a sufficient command of Spanish to get along in all ordinary situations.

The brief but complete summary of Spanish grammar is included in the back of this book to enable you to perfect your knowledge of Spanish. There are also many other helpful features, such as vocabulary tips, practice exercises, and verb charts. The special section on letter-writing will show you how to answer an invitation, make a business inquiry, and address an envelope properly. Just as important is the *Living Language*™ *Common Usage Dictionary*. This is included in the course primarily for use as a reference book, but it is a good idea to do as much browsing in it as possible. It contains the most common Spanish words with their meanings illustrated by everyday sentences and idiomatic expressions. The basic words—those you should learn from the start—are capitalized to make them easy to find.

Keep practicing your Spanish as much as possible. Once you are well along in the course, try reading Spanish magazines, newspapers, and books. Use your Spanish whenever you get a chance—with Spanish-speaking friends, with the waiter at a Spanish restaurant, with other students.

This course tries to make the learning of Spanish as easy and enjoyable as possible, but a certain amount of application is necessary. The cassettes and books that make up this course provide you with all the material you need; the instructions on the next page tell you what to do. The rest is up to you.

Course Material

The material of the complete Living Language Course® consists of the following:

1. *2 hour-long cassettes.* The label on each face indicates clearly which lessons are contained on that side. (Living Spanish is also available on 4 long-playing records.)

2. *Conversational Spanish book.* This book is designed for use with the recorded lessons, or it may be used alone. It contains the following sections:
   Basic Spanish Vocabulary and Grammar
   Summary of Spanish Grammar
   Verb Charts
   Letter-writing

3. *Spanish-English/English-Spanish Common Usage Dictionary.* A special kind of dictionary that gives you the literal translations of more than 20,000 Spanish words, plus idiomatic phrases and sentences illustrating the everyday use of the more important vocabulary and 1,000 essential words capitalized for ready reference.

How to Use Conversational Spanish with the Living Language™ Cassettes

TO BEGIN
There are 2 cassettes with 10 lessons per side. The beginning of each lesson is announced on the tape and each lesson takes approximately 3 minutes. If your cassette player has a digit indicator, you can locate any desired point precisely.

LEARNING THE LESSONS

1. Look at page 1. Note the words in **boldface** type. These are the words you will hear on the cassette. There are pauses to enable you to repeat each word and phrase right after you hear it.

2. Now read Lesson 1. (The ▭ ▭ symbols indicate the beginning of the recorded material. In some advanced lessons, information and instructions precede the recording.) Note the points to listen for when you play the cassette. Look at the first word: **Alicia**, and be prepared to follow the voice you will hear.

3. Play the cassette, listen carefully, and watch for the points mentioned. Then rewind, play the lesson again, and this time say the words aloud. Keep repeating until you are sure you know the lesson. The more times you listen and repeat, the longer you will remember the material.

4. Now go on to the next lesson. It's always good to quickly review the previous lesson before starting a new one.

5. There are 2 kinds of quizzes at the end of each section. One is the matching type, in which you must select the English translation of the Spanish sentence. In the other, you fill in the blanks with the correct Spanish word chosen from the 3 given directly below the sentence. Do these quizzes faithfully and, if you make any mistakes, reread the section.

6. When you get 100 percent on the Final Quiz, you may consider that you have mastered the course.

Living Language™

CONVERSATIONAL
SPANISH

LESSON 1

1. THE LETTERS AND SOUNDS

(Letters and Sounds I)

A. Some Spanish sounds are like English. Listen to and repeat the following Spanish names and notice which sounds are similar and which are different:

Alicia[1]	Alice	**Luis**	Louis
Alfredo	Alfred	**Luisa**	Louise
Antonio	Anthony	**Manuel**	Emanuel
Carlos	Charles	**Miguel**	Michael
Carmen	Carmen	**María**	Mary
Enrique	Henry	**Pedro**	Peter
Elisa	Elizabeth	**Pablo**	Paul
Francisco	Francis	**Pepe**	Joe
Fernando	Ferdinand	**Pilar**	Pilar
Isabel	Elizabeth	**Rafael**	Ralph[2]
Juan	John	**Ramón**	Raymond
Juana	Jane	**Rosa**	Rose
Juanita	Jennie	**Ricardo**	Richard
Jorge	George	**Roberto**	Robert
Julio	Jules	**Vicente**	Vincent
Julia	Julia	**Violeta**	Violet
José	Joseph	**Virginia**	Virginia

NOTICE:

1. that each vowel is pronounced clearly and crisply.

2. that a single consonant is pronounced with the following vowel.

3. that the mark (˜) placed over the letter *n* indicates the sound *ni* in *onion* or *ny* in *canyon*.

---

[1] Words in bold face are on the tape.
[2] Or Raphael.

4. that the accent mark (´) shows the syllable that is stressed. Sometimes, however, it serves merely to distinguish words:

> *él* he and *el* the
> *sí* yes and *si* if

B. Now listen to some place names:

Barcelona
Buenos Aires ("good air")[1]
Colorado ("red")
Gibraltar
La Habana
Las Vegas ("the meadows")
Los Angeles ("the angels")
Madrid
Montana
Nevada ("snowfall")
Río Grande ("big river")
Río de Janeiro ("river of Janeiro")
Santa Fé
San Fernando
Sierra Nevada ("snow-covered mountain chain")
Tampico
Veracruz ("true cross")

C. Now the names of some countries:

Argentina
Brasil
Colombia
Cuba
Chile
Costa Rica ("rich coast")
Estados Unidos

---

[1]Words in quotation marks are literal translations.

España
Francia
Guatemala
Honduras
Inglaterra
México
Nicaragua
Puerto Rico ("rich port")
Panamá
Perú
Portugal
El Salvador
Venezuela

Notice the following points:

VOWELS

a	as in *ah*, *father*.
e	as in *day*, *ace*.
i	as in *machine*, *police*.
o	as in *no*, *note*.
u	as in *rule*.

CONSONANTS

h	is never pronounced.
ñ	is like *ni* in *onion* or *ny* in *canyon*.
r	is pronounced by tapping the tip of the tongue against the gum ridge back of the upper teeth.
rr	is pronounced the same way but rolled, like the telephone operator's "th-r-r-ee."
s	between vowels is always like *ss* in English *lesson*, never like the *s* (pronounced *z*) in rose.

NOTICE:

1. that words ending in a vowel, *n* or *s* are stressed on the syllable before last:

hora	hour
arte	art
hablan	they're talking
amigos	friends

2. that all other words are stressed on the last syllable or on the syllable which has the accent:

hotel	hotel
general	general
inglés	English
razón	reason
América	America

LESSON 2

D. Now listen to and repeat the following words which are similar in English and Spanish. Notice how Spanish spelling and pronunciation differ from English:

(Letters and Sounds II)

acción	action	**gala**	gala
agente	agent	**guitarra**	guitar
atención	attention	**importante**	important
caso	case	**interesante**	interesting
centro	center	**necesario**	necessary
cheque	check	**posible**	possible
cierto	certain	**quieto**	quiet
cuestión	question	**radio**	radio
diferente	different	**restaurante**	restaurant
difícil	difficult	**similar**	similar
ejemplo	example	**té**	tea

teatro	theater	**tren**	train
teléfono	telephone	**visita**	visit

Notice the following points:

1. *c* before *a* and *u* is like *k*:

caso   case

2. *c* before *e* and *i* is pronounced in Spain like the *th* in *thin*; in Latin America like the *s* in *see*:

Pronounced as in Spain	*Pronounced as in Latin America*	
cigarro	**cigarro**	cigar
cinco	**cinco**	five

3. *qu* is always followed by *e* or *i* and is pronounced *k*:

quieto   quiet

4. *cc* is always followed by *i*. The first *c* is like *k*, the second is pronounced in Spain like the *th* in *thin* and in South America like the *s* in *see*:

Pronounced as in Spain	*Pronounced as in Latin America*	
acción	**acción**	action

5. *cu* is like *qu* in *quick*:

cuestión   question

6. *ch* is like *ch* in *church*:

cheque   check

7. *g* before *a, o* and *u* is like *g* in *go*:

gala   gala

8. *g* before *e* and *i* is a very strong rasping *h*, like the sound you make when you clear your throat:

general   general

9. *j* is similar to *g* before *e* and *i*:

ejemplo   example

10. *gu* before *e* is like *g* in *go*:

guitarra   guitar

11. *gu* before *a, o* and *u* is like *gw*:

Guatemala   Guatemala

12. Two dots are written over the *u* in the combination *gu* when it is pronounced *gw*:

paragüero   umbrella man;
                           umbrella stand

13. *ll* has two pronunciations. In Spain it is pronounced like the *lli* in *million*; in Latin America it is pronounced like the *y* in *yes*;

Pronounced as in Spain	Pronounced as in Latin America	
millón	**millón**	million
villa	**villa**	villa
calle	**calle**	street

14. *z* is like *c* before *e* and *i*: that is, in Spain it is pronounced like the *th* in *thin* and in Latin America like the *s* in *see*:

Pronounced as in Spain	Pronounced as in Latin America	
plaza	**plaza**	plaza, square

2. THE SPANISH ALPHABET

Letter	Name	Letter	Name	Letter	Name
a	a	j	jota	r	ere
b	be	k	ka	rr	erre
c	ce	l	ele	s	ese
ch	che	ll	elle	t	te
d	de	m	eme	u	u
e	e	n	ene	v	ve
f	efe	ñ	eñe	w	doble ve
g	ge	o	o	x	equis
h	hache	p	pe	y	i-griega
i	i	q	cu	z	zeta

NOTICE:

1. that the order differs from the order of our alphabet.
2. that *ch, ll* and *rr* represent single sounds and are treated as one letter (that is, they are never divided).
3. that *ñ* is treated as a separate letter.
4. that the Spanish alphabet has 30 letters—four more than the English.

3. REGIONAL DIFFERENCES IN PRONUNCIATION

The Spanish of Central and Northern Spain[1] ("Castilian Spanish") is considered a sort of "standard" Spanish, somewhat the way Parisian French, for example, is considered "standard" French. If, therefore, you learn the Castilian pronunciation you can get along in every region where Spanish is spoken. However, since more Americans use their Spanish

[1]The Spanish of Southern Spain is in general like that of Latin America.

in Latin America than in Spain, Spanish-American pronunciation is of great practical importance. The American who expects to visit Latin America or do business with Latin-American firms might as well learn Spanish-American pronunciation from the start.[1]

There are a number of minor differences in pronunciation between the various Latin-American countries, but like the differences between Castilian and Latin-American Spanish, they are not very numerous. The most important regional differences are:

1. *c* before *e* and *i*

   In Spain *th* in *think*. In Latin America *ss* in *lesson*.

2. *ll*

   In Spain *lli* in *million*. In Latin America *y* in *yes*.

3. In Argentina, etc. *ll* and *y* are pronounced like the *s* in *measure* (at times like the *j* in *judge*).

4. In Puerto Rico, Chile, etc. *s* is in some cases completely dropped or is pronounced like an English *h* or a soft Spanish *j*:

   esto "this" becomes *e(h)-to*

5. In some regions the *d* in the ending *-ado* is silent:

   comprado "bought" becomes *compra-o*

6. In some regions final *n* is pronounced almost like the English *ng* in *sing*:

   bien "well" is almost *bieng*

---

[1] You will hear both the Castilian and Latin-American pronunciation on the tapes that accompany this course. Lessons 1-31 and 39-40 are recorded with the Latin-American pronunciation; Lessons 26, 32-34 and 37 are recorded with the Castilian pronunciation. The remaining tapes contain conversations in which some speakers use the Latin-American and others the Castilian pronunciation.

LESSON 3

4. PRONUNCIATION PRACTICE

(Pronunciation Practice I)

The following groups of words will give you some additional practice in Spanish pronunciation and spelling:

VOWELS

1. *a* is like *ah* or the *a* in *father*:

a	to, at	**las**	the (*fem. pl.*)
amigo	friend	**pan**	bread
la	the (*fem. sg.*)	**habla**	he (*or* she) is speaking

2. *e* is like the *ay* in *day* but cut off sharply (that is, not drawled):

el	the	**carne**	meat
de	of	**tren**	train
en	in	**tres**	three
padre	father	**este**	this
se	itself		

Notice that when *e* comes at the end of a word or syllable it is close to the *ay* in *day* (but cut off sharply). Otherwise it is closer to our *e* in *ten*.

3. *i* is like the *i* in *police, machine, marine* but not drawled:

mí	me	**hijo**	son
sí	yes	**muy**	very
amiga	friend (*fem.*)	**hoy**	today

When it follows a vowel or stands by itself, *y* is pronounced like the Spanish *i*: *muy* "very," *y* "and." Otherwise it is like the English *y*: *yo* "I."

4. *o* is like the *o* in *no* but not drawled:

no	no	**ocho**	eight
dos	two	**cómo**	how
hora	hour	**febrero**	February
con	with		

Notice that when *o* comes at the end of a word or syllable it sounds like the *o* in *no* (but cut off sharply). Otherwise it is closer to the *o* in *north*.

5. *u* is as in *rule* but not drawled:

uno	one (*masc.*)	**tú**	you (*familiar*)
una	one (*fem.*)	**mucho**	much

6. Notice that each vowel is clearly pronounced. Vowels are not slurred over as they often are in English:

Europa	Europe	**idea**	idea
leer	to read	**peor**	worse
hay	there is, there are	**día**	day
ahí	there	**mío**	my
soy	I am	**país**	country

7. Common vowel combinations:

a. *ai, ay*

aire	air	**hay**	there is, there are

b. *au*

restaurante	restaurant	**automóvil**	automobile
autobús	bus		

c. *ei, ey*

seis	six	**ley**	law
treinta	thirty		

d. *ia, ya*

gracias	thanks	estudiar	to study
comercial	commercial	ya	already

e. *ie, ye*

pie	foot	bien	well
siete	seven	quien	who
quiero	I want	cien	hundred
tiene	he has	siempre	always
diez	ten	yerba	grass

f. *io, yo*

despacio	slowly	acción	action
estación	station	yo	I

g. *iu, yu*

ciudad	city	yuca	yucca plant

h. *oi, oy*

estoy	I am	voy	I'm going
hoy	today	doy	I give

i. *ua*

Juan	John	¿Cuánto?	How much?
¿Cuál?	Which?	cuatro	four

LESSON 4

(Pronunciation Practice II)

j. *ue*

nueve	nine	puerta	door
fuego	fire		

k. *uo*

continuo	continuous	antiguo	old

l. *ui, uy*

muy	very	ruido	noise
¡Cuidado!	Careful!		

CONSONANTS

1. *b* and *v*. Most Spanish speakers pronounce both letters alike. At the beginning of a word and after *m* or *n* they pronounce both *b* and *v* like English *b*:

bueno	good	**veinte**	twenty
vaso	glass	**hombre**	man

When *b* and *v* come between vowels they pronounce them somewhat like English *v*:

Cuba	Cuba	**haber**	to have
La Habana	Havana		

The sound differs from our *v* in that, instead of bringing the lower lip against the upper teeth, you bring the two lips together, the way you do when blowing dust from something.

However, some Spanish speakers pronounce *b* and *v* the way we do in English: they pronounce *b* whenever a *b* occurs in the spelling and *v* whenever a *v* occurs in the spelling:

vivir	to live	**beber**	to drink

2. *c* before consonants and the vowels *a, o* and *u* is pronounced *k*:

cosa	thing	**cuanto**	how much
casa	house		

—before *e* and *i* it is pronounced in Spain like the *th* in *thin* and in Latin America like the *s* in *see*:

cerca	near	**fácil**	easy
servicio	service	**docena**	dozen
cierto	certain		

3. *ch* is as in *church*:

mucho	much	**noche**	night
ocho	eight		

4. *d* is like the English *d* except that the tip of the tongue touches the back of the upper teeth. After a pause or after *n* it is pronounced like *d* in *day*:

día	day	**donde**	where
cuando	when		

—between vowels it is pronounced like *th* in *then*:

nada	nothing	**poder**	to be able
todo	all		

5. *f* is as in English:

familia   family

6. *g* is like the *g* in *go*:

grande   big, large

—before *a, o* and *u* it is like *g* in *go*:

lugar	place	**gusto**	pleasure

—before *e* and *i* it is like the Spanish *j* (a strong rasping *h*, somewhat like the sound you make when you clear your throat):

general	general	**Gibraltar**	Gibraltar

—*gu* is like the *g* in *go*:

guerra   war

7. *h* is never pronounced:

ahora	now	**hablo**	I speak

8. *j* is a strong rasping *h* (the same sound as *g* before *e* and *i*):

julio	July	**mejor**	better
jabón	soap		

9. *ll* is pronounced in Spain like the *lli* in *million*;
   in Latin America like the *y* in *yes*:

Pronounced as in Spain	*Pronounced as in Latin America*	
Me llamo...	**Me llamo...**	My name is ...
pollo	**pollo**	chicken

10. *m* is as in English:

mismo   the same

11. *n* is as in English:

nunca   never

12. *ñ* is like the *ni* in *onion* or the *ny* in *canyon*:

español   Spanish   **mañana**   tomorrow

13. *p* is as in English:

para   for

14. *qu* is like the English *k*:

¿Qué?   What?

15. *r* is made by tapping the tip of the tongue
    against the gum ridge back of the upper teeth,
    somewhat like British "veddy" for "very":

América   America

16. *rr* is made by trilling the tip of the tongue
    against the gum ridge back of the upper teeth,
    like the telephone operator's "th-r-r-ee":

cigarrillo   cigarette

When *r* comes at the beginning of a word it is pronounced like *rr*:

rico   rich

Listen to the following words, the first of which has *r*, the second *rr*:

pero	but	**perro**	dog
caro	dear	**carro**	car; cart

17. *s* is like the *s* in *see* or the *ss* in *lesson* (never as in *rose*):

casa   house

18. *t* is as in English except that the tip of the tongue touches the back of the upper teeth:

fruta   fruit

19. *y* is as in *yes*:

ayer   yesterday

y meaning "and" is pronounced like *i* (see page 9):

norte y sur   north and south

20. *z* is like *c* before *e* and *i*; that is, it is pronounced in Spain like the *th* in *thin* and in Latin America like the *s* in *see*:

Pronounced as in Spain	*Pronounced as in Latin America*	
diez	**diez**	ten
voz	**voz**	voice
luz	**luz**	light
marzo	**marzo**	March
azul	**azul**	blue
razón	**razón**	reason

5. BUILDING UP A VOCABULARY

Building up a Spanish vocabulary is a rather easy matter since a great number of words are similar in English and Spanish. Many words are spelled exactly the same (though they may differ considerably in pronunciation):

Spanish	English	Spanish	English
actor	actor	gas	gas
animal	animal	general	general
auto	auto	hospital	hospital
capital	capital	hotel	hotel
central	central	humor	humor
cereal	cereal	idea	idea
chocolate	chocolate	local	local
color	color	material	material
doctor	doctor	motor	motor
familiar	familiar	original	original
personal	personal	simple	simple
probable	probable	terrible	terrible
regular	regular	total	total
similar	similar	usual	usual

There are many Spanish words which you will have no difficulty in recognizing despite minor differences. Some of these differences are:

a. The Spanish word has an accent mark:

área	area	melón	melon
conclusión	conclusion	ómnibus	omnibus
cónsul	consul	religión	religion

b. The Spanish word has a single consonant:

antena	antenna	inteligible	intelligible
anual	annual	ocasional	occasional
comercial	commercial	oficial	official
imposible	impossible	posible	possible
intelectual	intellectual	profesional	professional

c. The Spanish word adds -a, -e or -o:

lista	list	*parte*	part
mapa	map	*líquido*	liquid
problema	problem	*portero*	porter
persona	person	*producto*	product
coste	cost	*restaurante*	restaurant

d. The Spanish word ends in *a* or *o*, the English word in *e*:

causa	cause	*estado*	state
figura	figure	*estilo*	style
medicina	medicine	*favorito*	favorite
nota	note	*minuto*	minute
práctica	practice	*tubo*	tube
rosa	rose	*uso*	use

e. The Spanish word is slightly different in other respects:

automóvil	automobile	*especial*	special
cuestión	question	*origen*	origin

GENERAL EQUIVALENTS

1. Spanish *c (qu)* = English *k (ck)*:

franco	frank	*parque*	park
saco	sack	*ataque*	attack

2. Spanish *f* = English *ph*:

frase	phrase, sentence	*físico*	physical
		teléfono	telephone

3. Spanish *j* = English *x*:

ejecutar	execute	*ejemplo*	example
ejercicio	exercise	*fijar*	fix
Méjico	Mexico		

4. Spanish *t* = English *th*:

autor	author	*teatro*	theatre
autoridad	authority	*teoría*	theory
simpatía	sympathy		

5. Spanish *z* = English *ce*:

comenzar	commence	*raza*	race
fuerza	force		

6. Spanish *i* = English *y*:

estilo	style	*sistema*	system
misterio	mystery	*ritmo*	rhythm

7. Spanish *o* and *u* = English *ou*:

hora	hour	*sonido*	sound
corte	court	*sopa*	soup
montaña	mountain	*fundar*	found
anunciar	announce	*curso*	course

8. Spanish *ia* and *io* = English *y*:

compañía	company	*secretaria*	secretary
familia	family	*remedio*	remedy
historia	history	*territorio*	territory

9. Spanish *ia* and *io* = English *e*:

ausencia	absence	*policía*	police
diferencia	difference	*comercio*	commerce
distancia	distance	*edificio*	edifice,
experiencia	experience		building
noticia	notice	*silencio*	silence
justicia	justice	*servicio*	service

10. Spanish *ción* = English *tion*:

acción	action	*conversación*	conversation
atracción	attraction	*descripción*	description

| *estación* | station | *satisfacción* | satisfaction |
| *información* | information | *vacación* | vacation |

11. Spanish *o* = English *al*:

| *eléctrico* | electric(al) | *politico* | political |
| *eterno* | eternal | *práctico* | practical |

12. Spanish *oso* = English *ous*:

| *delicioso* | delicious | *numeroso* | numerous |
| *famoso* | famous | *religioso* | religious |

LESSON 5

6. USEFUL WORD GROUPS

(Useful Word Groups I)

NUMBERS

uno	one
dos	two
tres	three
cuatro	four
cinco	five
seis	six
siete	seven
ocho	eight
nueve	nine
diez	ten

THE DAYS OF THE WEEK

lunes	Monday
martes	Tuesday
miércoles	Wednesday
jueves	Thursday
viernes	Friday
sábado	Saturday
domingo	Sunday

THE MONTHS

enero	January
febrero	February
marzo	March
abril	April
mayo	May
junio	June
julio	July
agosto	August
septiembre	September
octubre	October
noviembre	November
diciembre	December

SOME COLORS

rojo	red
azul	blue
verde	green
negro	black
blanco	white
amarillo	yellow
café	brown (coffee color)
castaño	brown (chestnut color)
gris	gray

THE SEASONS

la primavera	spring
el verano	summer
el otoño	autumn
el invierno	winter

NORTH, SOUTH, EAST, WEST

norte	north
sur	south
este	east
oeste	west

MORNING, NOON AND NIGHT

mañana	morning
mediodía	noon
tarde	afternoon
noche	evening, night

TODAY, YESTERDAY, TOMORROW

hoy	today
ayer	yesterday
mañana	tomorrow

Hoy es viernes.	Today is Friday.
Ayer fué jueves.	Yesterday was Thursday.
Mañana es sábado.	Tomorrow is Saturday.
Uno y uno son dos.	One and one are two.
Uno y dos son tres.	One and two are three.
Dos y dos son cuatro.	Two and two are four.
Dos y tres son cinco.	Two and three are five.
Tres y tres son seis.	Three and three are six.
Tres y cuatro son siete.	Three and four are seven.
Cuatro y cuatro son ocho.	Four and four are eight.
Cuatro y cinco son nueve.	Four and five are nine.
Cinco y cinco son diez.	Five and five are ten.

QUIZ 1

Try matching these two columns:

1.	viernes	1.	January
2.	otoño	2.	summer
3.	jueves	3.	June
4.	primavera	4.	winter
5.	ocho	5.	October
6.	enero	6.	white
7.	invierno	7.	autumn
8.	verde	8.	Sunday
9.	junio	9.	eight
10.	verano	10.	spring
11.	lunes	11.	west
12.	cuatro	12.	Thursday
13.	octubre	13.	four
14.	domingo	14.	ten
15.	oeste	15.	red
16.	rojo	16.	black
17.	negro	17.	green
18.	diez	18.	Friday
19.	blanco	19.	gray
20.	gris	20.	Monday

ANSWERS

1—18; 2—7; 3—12; 4—10; 5—9; 6—1; 7—4; 8—17; 9—3; 10—2; 11—20; 12—13; 13—5; 14—8; 15—11; 16—15; 17—16; 18—14; 19—6; 20—19.

LESSON 6

7. GOOD MORNING!

(Good Morning!)

Por la mañana	In the Morning
buenos	good *(pl.)*
días	days
Buenos días	Good morning.
señor	Mr.
García	García
Buenos días, señor García.	Good morning, Mr. García.
cómo	how
está	are
usted	you
¿Cómo está usted?	How are you? How do you do?
muy	very
bien	well
Muy bien.	Very well.
gracias	thank you, thanks
Muy bien, gracias.	Very well, thank you.
y	and
usted	you
¿Y usted?	And how are you? ("And you?")
regular	fine
Regular, gracias.	Fine, thank you.

Por la tarde	In the Afternoon
buenas	good *(fem. pl.)*
tardes	afternoon ("afternoons")
Buenas tardes.	Good afternoon.

Por la tarde	In the Afternoon
Buenas tardes, señora de García.	Good afternoon, Mrs. García.
muy	very
buenas	good
tardes	afternoon
Muy buenas tardes, señor López.	Good afternoon, Mr. López.
cómo	how
se encuentra	find yourself
usted	you
¿Cómo se encuentra usted?	How are you?
perfectamente	fine ("perfectly")
y	and
usted	you
Perfectamente, ¿y usted?	Fine, and how are you?
yo	I
sin	without
novedad	anything new
Yo sin novedad, gracias.	Very well, thanks. Same as usual, thanks.

Al anochecer y de noche	In the Evening and at Night
muy	very
buenas	good
noches	night ("nights")
Muy buenas noches, señorita García.	Good evening (Good night), Miss García.
muy	very
buenas	good

noches	night
Muy buenas noches, Don Pedro.	Good evening (Good night), Don Pedro.
Muy buenas noches, Don Pedro García.	Good evening (Good night), Don Pedro García.

Note: *Señor* is the general term of address; *Don* implies both respect and a certain degree of familiarity. *Don Pedro* is more familiar than *Don Pedro García*. *Don* is never used before the second name alone: *Don Pedro* or *Don Pedro García* but never *Don García*.

QUIZ 2

1. mañana	1. Good afternoon.
2. señora	2. How are you?
3. ¿Cómo está usted?	3. Miss
4. Muy bien.	4. morning
5. Buenos días.	5. Thank you.
6. Muy buenas noches.	6. Madam or Mrs.
7. ¿Cómo se encuentra usted?	7. Same as usual.
8. perfectamente	8. Sir or Mr.
9. Gracias.	9. How?
10. Sin novedad	10. Good morning.
11. senorita	11. in the evening.
12. Buenas tardes.	12. How are you?
13. ¿Cómo?	13. Very well.
14. señor	14. fine ("perfectly")
15. al anochecher	15. Good evening. (Good night).

ANSWERS

1—4; 2—6; 3—12; 4—13; 5—10; 6—15; 7—2;
8—14; 9—5; 10—7; 11—3; 12—1; 13—9; 14—8;
15—11.

8. WHERE IS . . . ?

dónde	where
hay	there is
¿Dónde hay . . . ?	Where is there . . . ?
un	a
hotel	hotel
¿Dónde hay un hotel?	Where's there a hotel?
buen	good
restaurante	restaurant
¿Dónde hay un buen restaurante?	Where's there a good restaurant?
dónde	where
está	is
¿Dónde está?	Where is it?
¿Dónde está el teléfono?	Where's the telephone?
¿Dónde está el restaurante?	Where's the restaurant?
¿Dónde está la estación?	Where's the railroad station?
¿Dónde está el correo?	Where's the post office?

LESSON 7

(What Do You Have To Eat?)

puede usted	can you
decirme	tell me
¿Puede usted decirme . . . ?	Can you tell me . . . ?
¿Puede usted decirme dónde hay un hotel?	Can you tell me where there is a hotel?

¿Puede usted decirme dónde hay un buen restaurante?[1]	Can you tell me where there is a good restaurant?
¿Puede usted decirme dónde está el teléfono?	Can you tell me where the telephone is?
¿Puede usted decirme dónde está la estación?	Can you tell me where the station is?
¿Puede usted decirme dónde está el correo?	Can you tell me where the post office is?

QUIZ 3

1. ¿Dónde hay un hotel?	1. Where's the telephone?
2. ¿Dónde está el teléfono?	2. Can you tell me where the station is?
3. ¿Puede usted decirme . . . ?	3. Can you tell me . . . ?
4. ¿Puede usted decirme dónde está la estación?	4. the post office
5. el correo	5. Where is there a hotel?

ANSWERS

1—5; 2—1; 3—3; 4—2; 5—4.

9. DO YOU HAVE . . . ?

¿Tiene usted . . . ?	Do you have . . . ?
dinero	(any) money
cigarrillos	(any) cigarettes
fósforos	(any) matches
fuego	a light

[1]Notice that there are two common spellings and pronunciations: *restaurant* and *restaurante*.

Necesito . . .	I need . . .
papel	(some) paper
lápiz	(a) pencil
tinta	ink
un sello de correo	a stamp
jabón	soap
pasta dentífrica	toothpaste
una toalla	a towel
¿Dónde puedo comprar . . . ?	Where can I buy . . . ?
un diccionario español	a Spanish dictionary
un diccionario inglés-español	an English-Spanish dictionary
unos libros en inglés	some English books ("some books in English")
ropa	(some) clothes

10. WHAT DO YOU HAVE TO EAT?

desayuno	breakfast
almuerzo	lunch
comida	dinner, supper
¿Qué desea usted?	What will you have? ("What do you wish?")
déme	give me
el menú	the menu
por favor	please
Déme el menú, por favor.	May I have a menu, please?
Tráigame . . .	Bring me . . .
un poco de pan	(some) bread

pan y mantequilla	bread and butter
sopa	soup
carne	meat
carne de vaca	beef
biftec	steak
jamón	ham
pescado	fish
pollo	chicken
huevos	eggs
legumbres	vegetables
patatas	potatoes
ensalada	salad
agua	water
vino	wine
cerveza	beer
leche	milk
café con leche	coffee with milk
azúcar	sugar
sal	salt
pimienta	pepper
fruta	fruit
postre	dessert

Tráigame . . .	Bring me . . .
una taza de café	a cup of coffee
una taza de té	a cup of tea
una servilleta	a napkin
una cuchara	a spoon
una cucharita[1]	a teaspoon
una cucharilla[1]	a teaspoon
un cuchillo	a knife
un plato	a plate
un vaso	a glass

[1]*Cucharilla* is the more common word in Spain, *cucharita* the more common in Latin America.

Quisiera . . .	I would like . . .
un poco de fruta	some fruit
una botella de vino	a bottle of wine
una botella de vino tinto	a bottle of red wine
una botella de vino blanco	a bottle of white wine
otra botella de vino	another bottle of wine
un poco más de eso	a little more of that
un poco más de pan	a little more bread
un poco más de carne	a little more meat
La cuenta, por favor.	The check, please.

QUIZ 4

1. *carne*	1. fish
2. *patatas*	2. water
3. *agua*	3. vegetables
4. *¿Qué desea usted?*	4. I need soap.
5. *huevos*	5. The check, please.
6. *pollo*	6. breakfast
7. *pescado*	7. a spoon
8. *una botella de vino*	8. coffee with milk
9. *Necesito jabón.*	9. What will you have?
10. *Tráigame un poco de pan.*	10. dessert
11. *café con leche*	11. meat
12. *azúcar*	12. a knife
13. *legumbres*	13. eggs
14. *una taza de té*	14. Bring me some bread.
15. *un poco más de pan*	15. chicken
16. *un cuchillo*	16. a cup of tea
17. *postre*	17. some more bread
18. *desayuno*	18. sugar
19. *una cuchara*	19. a bottle of wine
20. *La cuenta, por favor.*	20. potatoes

ANSWERS

1—11; 2—20; 3—2; 4—9; 5—13; 6—15; 7—1;
8—19; 9—4; 10—14; 11—8; 12—18; 13—3; 14—16;
15—17; 16—12; 17—10; 18—6; 19—7; 20—5.

LESSON 8[1]

11. SOME COMMON VERB FORMS

(May I Introduce?)

yo hablo	I speak
tú hablas	you speak *(familiar)*
él habla	he speaks
ella habla	she speaks
usted habla	you speak *(polite)*
nosotros hablamos	we speak *(masc.)*
nosotras hablamos	we speak *(fem.)*
vosotros habláis	you speak *(masc.)*
vosotras habláis	you speak *(fem.)*
ellos hablan	they speak *(masc.)*
ellas hablan	they speak *(fem.)*
ustedes hablan	you speak *(polite)*

(Tape continued on page 38.)

NOTES

1. These forms, which make up the present tense,
   translate English "I speak," "I am speaking,"
   "I do speak."

[1]This lesson and several of the following lessons are longer than the
others. They contain the grammatical information you need to
know from the start. Don't try to memorize anything. Read each
section until you understand every point and then as you continue
with the course try to observe examples of the points mentioned.
Refer back to the grammatical sections as often as necessary. In this
way you will eventually find that you have a good grasp of the basic
features of Spanish grammar without any deliberate memorizing of
"rules."

2. *Tú* "you" is used to address people you know very well (whom you call by their first names in English—relatives, close friends, etc.) and to children, pets, etc. The plural is *vosotros* (fem. *vosotras*) but in many places in Spanish America the polite form *ustedes* is used even to close friends. *Tú* is called the "familiar" form, *usted* the "polite" or "formal."

3. Notice that there are six endings:

   Singular
   —o   indicates the speaker (I).
   —as   indicates the person spoken to (you). It is only used to someone you know well.
   —a   indicates someone or something spoken about (he, she, it) or else you *(polite)*.

   Plural
   —amos   indicates several people (we).
   —ais   indicates the persons spoken to (you). It is used only to people you know well.
   —an   indicates they (both masculine and feminine) or you *(polite)*.

4. Notice that the verb form with *usted, él* and *ella* is the same: *habla.*

5. The pronouns *yo, tú, él, ella,* etc. are not ordinarily used. "I speak" is just *hablo,* "we speak" is *hablamos,* the *-o* and *-amos* being sufficient to indicate "I," "we," etc. The pronouns are used only for emphasis or clearness (i.e. *usted habla* "you speak" and *él habla* "he speaks").

6. Notice that several forms of the pronouns differ depending on whether men or women are speaking or are being spoken to or about.[1]

él habla	he is speaking
ella habla	she is speaking
nosotros hablamos	we are speaking *(men)*
nosotras hablamos	we are speaking *(women)*
vosotros habláis	you *(fam.)* are speaking *(men)*
vosotras habláis	you *(fam.)* are speaking *(women)*
ellos hablan	they are speaking *(men)*
ellas hablan	they are speaking *(women)*

7. *Usted* (abbreviated *Ud.*[2]) and *ustedes* (*Uds.*) are abbreviations of *vuestra merced*, "Your Grace" (plural: *vuestras mercedes*) and therefore take the third person form: *¿Cómo está usted?*

12. THE AND A

1. The

el muchacho	the boy	*los muchachos*	the boys
la muchacha	the girl	*las muchachas*	the girls

Notice that the word for "the" is in some cases *el* (plural: *los*), in other cases *la* (plural: *las*). Nouns that take *el* are called "masculine,"

[1]This is also true when the pronouns refer to masculine or feminine nouns (see page 229).
[2]The abbreviation *Ud.* (*Uds.*) is used in Latin America; in Spain the form is commonly abbreviated *Vd.* (*Vds.*) or *V.* (*V.V.*).

nouns that take *la* are called "feminine." Nouns referring to males are masculine, nouns referring to females are feminine. In the case of other nouns you have to learn whether the noun is masculine (that is, takes *el*) or feminine (that is, takes *la*).

Lo "the" is used before parts of speech other than nouns when they are used as nouns:

lo pasado	the past, what is past
lo necesario	the necessary thing
lo dicho	what is said

2. A (An)

un muchacho	a boy
una muchacha	a girl

unos muchachos	boys, some (a few) boys
unas muchachas	girls, some (a few) girls

Unos (unas) is often used where we would use "some" or "a few" in English: *unos días,* "a few days."

QUIZ 5

1.	*yo*	1.	they speak
2.	*nosotros*	2.	she is speaking
3.	*usted habla*	3.	she
4.	*él*	4.	you *(fam. plural)*
5.	*ellos hablan*	5.	I
6.	*vosotros*	6.	you speak
7.	*tú*	7.	he
8.	*ella*	8.	we speak *(women)*
9.	*nosotras hablamos*	9.	you *(fam. sing.)*
10.	*ella habla*	10.	we

ANSWERS

1—5; 2—10; 3—6; 4—7; 5—1; 6—4; 7—9; 8—3; 9—8; 10—2.

13. CONTRACTIONS

de + el = del   of the, from the
a + el = al   to the

del muchacho   of (from) the boy
al muchacho   to the boy

14. PLURAL

1. To form the plural you add -*s*:

el libro	the book	*los libros*	the books
la carta	the letter	*las cartas*	the letters

2. If the noun ends in a consonant you add -*es*:

el avión   the airplane *los aviones* the airplanes

3. If the noun ends in -*z* you change the *z* to *c* and then add -*es*:

la luz   the light   *las luces*   the lights

15. ADJECTIVES

un muchacho alto   a tall boy
una muchacha alta   a tall girl

unos muchachos altos   tall boys
unas muchachas altas   tall girls

Notice that the adjective follows the noun and has the same form (that is, is masculine if the noun is masculine, plural if the noun is plural, etc.).

When the adjective is used by itself, its form tells you whether the reference is to men (or masculine nouns) or to women (or feminine nouns) and whether it is to one person (or thing) or to several:

(él) Es español.	He's Spanish.
(ella) Es española.	She's Spanish.
(ellos) Son españoles.	They're Spanish *(masc.).*
(ellas) Son españolas.	They're Spanish *(fem.).*

16. POSSESSION

English -*'s* or *-s'* is translated by *de* "of":

el libro de Juan	John's book ("the book of John")
los libros de los muchachos	the boys' books ("the books of the boys")

17. ASKING A QUESTION

1. To ask a question you put the subject after the verb:

Usted ha comido.	You have eaten.
¿Ha comido usted?	Have you eaten?

2. Adjectives come right after the verb:

¿Es fácil el español?	Is Spanish easy?

18. NOT

The word for "not" is *no*. It comes before the verb:

No veo.	I don't see.

REVIEW QUIZ 1

1. *Buenos* _____ (afternoon), *señora de Garcia.*
   - a. *mañana*
   - b. *tardes*
   - c. *gracias*

2. *¿Puede usted decirme* _____ (where) *está el correo?*
   - a. *dónde*
   - b. *buen*
   - c. *allá*

3. _____ (bring me) *un poco de pan.*
   - a. *desea*
   - b. *tomar*
   - c. *tráigame*

4. *Café con* _____ (milk).
   - a. *azúcar*
   - b. *vino*
   - c. *leche*

5. *Un poco* _____ (more) *de carne.*
   - a. *más*
   - b. *taza*
   - c. *otra*

6. *El siete de* _____ (January).
   - a. *marzo*
   - b. *enero*
   - c. *agosto*

7. _____ (Wednesday), *cinco de septiembre.*
   - a. *viernes*
   - b. *sábado*
   - c. *miércoles*

8. ¿ _____ (how) *está usted?*
   a. *gracias*
   b. *cómo*
   c. *tardes*

9. *Muy buenas* _____ (night), *señorita García.*
   a. *sin*
   b. *noches*
   c. *yo*

10. *Quisiera una botella de* _____ (wine).
    a. *leche*
    b. *vino*
    c. *agua*

ANSWERS

1 b.; 2 a.; 3 c.; 4 c.; 5 a.; 6 b.; 7 c.; 8 b.; 9 b.; 10 b.

19. MAY I INTRODUCE . . . ?

Buenos días.	Good morning.
Buenos días, señor.	Good morning (sir).
¿Cómo está usted?	How are you?
Muy bien, gracias. ¿Y usted? ¿Es usted norteamericano?	Very well, thanks. How are you? Are you from the United States?
Sí, señor.	Yes (sir).
¿Habla usted español?	Do you speak Spanish?
Un poco.	A little.
le presento	I present you
a mi amiga	to my friend
la Señorita García	Miss García

Le presento a mi amiga, la Señorita García.	May I introduce my friend, Miss García?
mucho gusto en conocerla	much pleasure in knowing you
Mucho gusto en conocerla.	I'm glad to know you.
el gusto es mío	the pleasure is mine
El gusto es mío.	The pleasure is mine.
permita usted que me presente Juan García para servirle	permit that I introduce myself John García at your service ("to serve you")
Permita usted que me presente, Juan García, para servirle.	May I introduce myself? I'm John García.
Manuel Fernández a sus órdenes	Manuel Fernández at your service ("at you orders")
Manuel Fernández, a sus órdenes.[1]	I'm Manuel Fernández.
permítame presentarle a mi amigo	allow me to present you to my friend
Permítame presentarle a mi amigo el doctor Pérez.	Allow me to introduce you to my friend Dr. Pérez.

[1]Notice the use of *para servirle* and *a sus órdenes*. There are many of these polite expressions in Spanish for which there are no English equivalents.

tanto	so much
gusto	pleasure
en	in
conocerle[1]	knowing you
Tanto gusto en conocerle, Dr. Pérez.	I'm very glad to know you, Dr. Pérez.
el gusto	the pleasure
es mío	is mine
El gusto es mío, señor.	The pleasure is mine, sir.

20. IT'S BEEN A REAL PLEASURE

he tenido	I've had
un verdadero	a real
gusto	pleasure
He tenido un verdadero gusto.	It's been a real pleasure.
el gusto	the pleasure
ha sido mío	has been mine.
El gusto ha sido mío.	The pleasure was mine.
Adiós.	Good-by.
hasta	until
otro	another
día	day
Hasta otro día.	See you soon.
Adiós. Hasta otro día.	Good-by. See you soon.
hasta	until
luego	later
Hasta luego.	So long. See you soon.

[1]Notice that you say *conocerla* when speaking to a woman *(see above)* and *conocerle* when speaking to a man.

hasta	until
la vista	the sight
Hasta la vista.	See you soon. So long.
Buenas noches.	Good night.
muy	very
buenas	good
Muy buenas.[1]	Good night.
Hasta mañana.	See you tomorrow.

LESSON 9

21. HOW ARE THINGS?

(How Are Things?)

¡Hola Manuel!	Hello, Manuel.
¡Hola Juan!	Hello, John.
¿Qué tal?	How are you? (How are things?)
Bien, ¿y tú?	Fine. And how are you?
qué	what
hay	is there
de	of
nuevo	new
¿Qué hay de nuevo?	What's new?
nada	nothing
de	of
particular	particular
Nada de particular.	Nothing in particular.

---

[1] *Muy buenas* is a very colloquial way of saying "Good night."

qué	what
me cuenta	do (you) tell me
usted	you
¿Qué me cuenta usted?	What's new?
poca	little
cosa	thing
Poca cosa.	Not much.

QUIZ 6

1. *¿Qué tal?*	1. Nothing in particular.
2. *Hasta luego.*	2. Allow me to introduce you to my friend.
3. *Buenas noches.*	3. See you soon.
4. *Hola Juan.*	4. Hello, John.
5. *Nada de particular.*	5. I'm very glad to know you.
6. *Permítame presentarle a mi amigo.*	6. How are you?
7. *Hasta la vista.*	7. Good night.
8. *nuevo*	8. to know you
9. *Tanto gusto en conocerle.*	9. new
10. *conocerle*	10. So long.

ANSWERS

1—6; 2—10; 3—7; 4—4; 5—1; 6—2; 7—3; 8—9; 9—5; 10—8.

22. TO BE OR NOT TO BE

There are two words in Spanish for "to be": *ser* and *estar*. In general *ser* indicates a permanent state (I'm an American), *estar* a temporary one (I'm tired).

SER

yo soy	I am
tú eres	you are
él es	he is
nosotros somos	we are
vosotros sois	you are
ellos son	they are

ESTAR

yo estoy	I am
tú estás	you are
él está	he is
nosotros estamos	we are
vosotros estáis	you are
ellos están	they are

SER

El es médico.	He's a doctor.
Es español.	He's a Spaniard.
Ella es joven.	She's young.
Es inteligente.	He's intelligent.
Soy yo.	It's me (I).
¿De dónde es usted?	Where are you from?
Soy de España.	I'm from Spain.
¿Es de madera?	Is it made of wood?
¿De quién es esto?	Whose is this?
Esto es de él.	This is his.
Es tarde.	It's late.
Es temprano.	It's early.
Es la una.	It's one o'clock.
Es necesario.	It's necessary.
Es lástima.	It's a pity. It's too bad.

ESTAR

Está allí.	He's over there.
Está en México.[1]	He's in Mexico.
¿Dónde está el libro?	Where's the book?
Está sobre la mesa.	It's on the table.
Estoy cansado.	I'm tired.
Estoy listo.	I'm ready.
El café está frío.	The coffee is cold.
Está claro.	It's clear. It's obvious.
La ventana está abierta.	The window is open.
La ventana está cerrada.	The window is shut.

QUIZ 7

1. *Es inteligente.*	1. Whose is this?
2. *Es lástima.*	2. Where are you from?
3. *El es médico.*	3. they are
4. *yo soy*	4. He's a doctor.
5. *Es la una.*	5. It's early.
6. *nosotros somos*	6. He's a Spaniard.
7. *Es de madera.*	7. He's intelligent.
8. *¿De dónde es usted?*	8. It's a pity.
9. *Está allí.*	9. I am
10. *Es temprano.*	10. It's one o'clock.
11. *Estoy cansado.*	11. It's made of wood.
12. *ellos están*	12. we are
13. *¿De quién es esto?*	13. He's over there.
14. *Es tarde.*	14. I'm tired.
15. *Es español.*	15. It's late.

ANSWERS

1—7; 2—8; 3—4; 4—9; 5—10; 6—12; 7—11; 8—2;
9—13; 10—5; 11—14; 12—3; 13—1; 14—15; 15—6.

---

[1]In the word *México* the *x* is pronounced as though it were written *j*.
Except in Mexico, the word is spelled with a *j*.

23. IT IS

Es . . .	It is . . .
Es verdad.	It's true.
Eso no es verdad.	That isn't true. That isn't so.
Está . . . [1]	It is . . .
Está bien.	It's all right.
No está bien.	It's not all right.
Es así.	It's so. That's the way it is.
Está mal.	It's bad.
Está muy mal.	It's very bad.
Es cierto.	It's certain.
Es grande.	It's big.
Es pequeño.	It's small.
Es caro.	It's expensive.
Es barato.	It's cheap.
Está cerca.	It's near.
Está lejos.	It's far.
Es difícil.	It's difficult.
Es fácil.	It's easy.
Es poco.	It's a little. It's not much.
Es muy poco.	It's very little.
Es mucho.	It's a lot.
Es bastante.	It's enough.
No es bastante.	It's not enough.
Está aquí.	It's here.
Está ahí.	It's there.
Es suyo.	It's yours.
Es mío.	It's mine.
Es nuestro.	It's ours.
Es para usted.	It's for you.

[1]For the difference between *es* and *está* see page 43.

QUIZ 8

1. *Es mucho.*	1. It's enough.
2. *Es fácil.*	2. That isn't true.
3. *Está cerca.*	3. It's bad.
4. *Es bastante.*	4. It's near.
5. *Eso no es verdad.*	5. It's mine.
6. *Está mal.*	6. It's true.
7. *Es pequeño.*	7. It's here.
8. *Es verdad.*	8. It's small.
9. *Es mío.*	9. It's easy.
10. *Está aquí.*	10. It's a lot.

ANSWERS

1—10; 2—9; 3—4; 4—1; 5—2; 6—3; 7—8; 8—6; 9—5; 10—7.

LESSON 10

24. TO HAVE AND HAVE NOT

(I Know Only A Little Spanish)

TO HAVE

yo tengo	I have
tú tienes	you have
él tiene	he has
nosotros tenemos	we have
vosotros tenéis	you have
ellos tienen	they have

NOT TO HAVE

yo no tengo	I don't have
tú no tienes	you don't have
él no tiene	he doesn't have
nosotros no tenemos	we don't have
vosotros no tenéis	you don't have
ellos no tienen	they don't have

Tengo tiempo.	I have time.
No tengo tiempo.	I haven't any time.
No tiene amigos.	He hasn't any friends.
¿Tiene usted un cigarrillo?	Do you have a cigarette?
Tengo hambre.	I'm hungry. ("I have hunger.")
Tengo sed.	I'm thirsty. ("I have thirst.")
Tengo frío.	I'm cold. ("I have cold.")
Tengo calor.	I'm warm. ("I have warmth.")
Tengo razón.	I'm right. ("I have reason.")

25. I KNOW ONLY A LITTLE SPANISH

¿Habla usted español?	Do you speak Spanish?
Sí, un poco.	Yes, a little.
Muy poco.	Very little.
No muy bien.	Not very well.
Hablo español.	I speak Spanish.
Lo hablo mal.	I speak it poorly.
No lo hablo muy bien.	I don't speak it very well.
Sólo sé unas cuantas palabras.	I only know a few words.
Sé decir algunas palabras en español.	I can say ("I know how to say") a few words in Spanish.
¿Habla su amigo español?	Does your friend speak Spanish?
No, mi amigo no habla español.	No, my friend doesn't speak Spanish.

¿Entiende usted el español?	Do you understand Spanish?
Sí, entiendo español.	Yes, I understand Spanish.
Lo entiendo pero no lo hablo.	I understand it but I don't speak it.
Lo leo pero no lo hablo.	I read it but I don't speak it.
No, no entiendo español.	No, I don't understand Spanish.
No entiendo muy bien el español.	I don't understand Spanish very well.
No lo pronuncio muy bien.	I don't pronounce it very well.
Me falta práctica.	I need practice. ("There is lacking to me practice.")
¿Me entiende usted?	Do you understand me?
Le entiendo.	I understand you.
No le entiendo muy bien.	I don't understand you very well.
¿Qué ha dicho usted?	What did you say?
Usted habla muy de prisa.	You speak too fast. You're speaking too fast.
No hable tan de prisa.	Don't speak so fast.
Hable más despacio.	Speak more slowly.
Tenga la bondad de hablar más despacio.	Please speak a little more slowly. ("Have the goodness to . . .")
Usted dispense, pero no le he entendido.	Excuse me but I don't understand. ("I didn't understand you.")
Repítamelo.	Please say it again ("to me").
¿Me entiende ahora?	Do you understand me now?

Ah, ya entiendo.	Oh, now I understand.
¿Qué quiere decir eso en español?	What does that mean in Spanish?
¿Cómo se dice "Thanks" en español?	How do you say "Thanks" in Spanish?
¿Cómo se escribe esa palabra?	How do you spell ("write") that word?
Escríbamela, por favor.	Please write it down for me.

LESSON 11

26. DO YOU SPEAK SPANISH?

(Do You Speak Spanish?)

Buenos días, señor.	Good morning, sir.
Buenos días.	Good morning.
¿Habla usted español?	Do you speak Spanish?
Sí, hablo español.	Yes, I speak Spanish.
No hablo inglés.	I don't speak English.
¿Es usted suramericano, señor?	Are you a Latin American?
Sí, soy chileno.	Yes, I'm from Chile. ("I'm a Chilean.")
¿Cuánto tiempo lleva usted en los Estados Unidos?	How long have you been in the United States?
Tres meses.	Three months.
Aprenderá inglés en poco tiempo. No es muy difícil.	You'll soon learn English. ("You'll learn English in little time.") It's not very hard.

Es más difícil de lo que usted se piensa.	It's harder than you think.
Quizás tenga usted razón. Para nosotros es más fácil aprender español[1] que para ustedes inglés.[1]	You're probably right. ("Perhaps you have reason.") Spanish is easier for us to learn than English is for you. ("For us it is easier to learn Spanish than for you English.")
Usted habla muy bien el español.	You speak Spanish very well.
Viví en México por varios años.	I lived in Mexico for several years.
Tiene usted una pronunciación muy buena.	You have an excellent pronunciation.
Muchas gracias. Sin embargo, necesito practicar.	Thank you. I need practice though. ("Nevertheless I need to practice.")
Tendré que marcharme. Va a salir mi tren.	I'll have to leave now. My train's about to leave. ("My train's going to go.")
Buena suerte y buen viaje.	Good luck and a pleasant trip.
Lo mismo le deseo a usted.	The same to you. ("I wish you the same.")
Adiós	Good-by.

---

[1] *El español* and *el inglés* are also correct to use.

QUIZ 9

1. *Lo entiendo pero no lo hablo.*	1. Do you speak Spanish?
2. *¿Me entiende ahora?*	2. I need practice.
3. *No lo hablo muy bien.*	3. a little
4. *Usted habla muy de prisa.*	4. What did you say?
5. *¿Cómo se escribe esa palabra?*	5. Please say it again.
6. *¿Habla usted español?*	6. not very well
7. *Necesito practicar.*	7. I didn't understand you very well.
8. *un poco*	8. I understand it but I don't speak it.
9. *Repítamelo.*	9. Speak more slowly.
10. *no muy bien*	10. I don't speak it very well.
11. *Hable más despacio.*	11. How do you say "Thanks" in Spanish?
12. *Lo hablo mal.*	12. You speak too fast.
13. *¿Qué ha dicho usted?*	13. Do you understand me now?
14. *¿Cómo se dice "Thanks" en español?*	14. How do you spell that word?
15. *No le he entendido muy bien.*	15. I speak it poorly.

ANSWERS

1—8; 2—13; 3—10; 4—12; 5—14; 6—1; 7—2; 8—3; 9—5; 10—6; 11—9; 12—15; 13—4; 14—11; 15—7.

27. EXCUSE ME

Perdón.	Pardon me. Excuse me.
Perdone usted.	I beg your pardon.
Dispense usted.	Excuse me.
¿Me hace el favor de repetirlo?	Please repeat. ("Will you do me the favor of repeating it?")
Con gusto.	With pleasure. Gladly.
Con mucho gusto.	With great pleasure. Very gladly.
Con muchísimo gusto.	With the greatest pleasure.
Estoy a sus órdenes.	I'm at your disposal ("orders").
¿En qué puedo servirle?	What can I do for you? ("In what can I serve you?")
Usted es muy amable.	You're very kind. That's very kind of you.
Usted es muy atento.	You're very kind. That's very kind of you.
Gracias.	Thanks.
Muchas gracias.	Many thanks.
Muchísimas gracias.	Thanks a lot. ("Very many thanks.")
Un millón de gracias.	Thanks very much. ("A million thanks.")
De nada.	Don't mention it.
No hay de qué.	Don't mention it.
No es nada.	It's nothing.

LESSON 12

28. THIS AND THAT

(This and That)

Dame éste.	Give me this one *(masc.)*.
Dame ésta.	Give me this one *(fem.)*.
Dame éstos.	Give me these *(masc.)*.
Dame éstas.	Give me these *(fem.)*.
Dame ése.	Give me that one *(masc.)*.
Dame ésa.	Give me that one *(fem.)*.
Dame ésos.	Give me those *(masc.)*.
Dame ésas.	Give me those *(fem.)*.
Dame aquél.	Give me that one over there *(refers to something farther away)*.
Dame aquélla.	Give me that one *(fem.)* over there.
Dame aquéllos.	Give me those over there.
Dame aquéllas.	Give me those *(fem.)* over there.

These forms also come before nouns:

este muchacho	this boy
esta señora	this lady
esa señora	that lady
aquél señor	that gentleman over there
aquéllos vecinos	those neighbors

QUIZ 10

1. *Dame éstos.*	1. Give me those over there.
2. *Éste.*	2. That one over there.
3. *Dame ésa.*	3. That lady.
4. *Este muchacho.*	4. This one.
5. *Ése.*	5. That gentleman over there.
6. *Aquéllos vecinos.*	6. This boy.
7. *Dame aquéllos.*	7. Give me these.
8. *Aquél.*	8. That one.
9. *Esta señora.*	9. Those neighbors.
10. *Aquél señor.*	10. Give me that one *(fem.)*.

ANSWERS

1—7; 2—4; 3—10; 4—6; 5—8; 6—9; 7—1; 8—2; 9—3; 10—5.

29. MORE OR LESS

1. More

más despacio	more slowly
más difícil	more difficult
más fácil	easier
más lejos	farther
más cerca	nearer
más que eso	more than that
más de un año	more than a year

2. Less

menos despacio	less slowly
menos difícil	less difficult
menos fácil	less easy
menos lejos	less far, not so far
menos cerca	less near, not so near
menos que eso	less than that
menos de un año	less than a year

REVIEW QUIZ 2

1. _____ (this) *muchacho.*
   - a. esta
   - b. este
   - c. esa

2. *Dame* _____ (those *fem.*).
   - a. ésas
   - b. éstos
   - c. aquél

3. *Tengo* _____ (here) *los libros.*
   - a. eso
   - b. aquí
   - c. como

4. *Venga usted* _____ (here).
   - a. pero
   - b. sino
   - c. acá

5. *Mañana voy* _____ (there).
   - a. allá
   - b. aquí
   - c. y

6. ¿ _____ (where) *está?*
   - a. aquí
   - b. dónde
   - c. cómo

7. *Está* _____ (far) *de aquí.*
   - a. lejos
   - b. cerca
   - c. allí

8. *Roberto* _____ (and) *Juan son hermanos.*
   a. *e*
   b. *y*
   c. *pero*

9. *Cinco* _____ (or) *seis pesos.*
   a. *o*
   b. *sino*
   c. *y*

10. *Quiero venir* _____ (but) *no puedo.*
    a. *o*
    b. *pero*
    c. *sino*

ANSWERS

1 b.; 2 a.; 3 b.; 4 c.; 5 a.; 6 b.; 7 a.; 8 b.; 9 a.; 10 b.

30. AND AND BUT

1. *y* "and"

Roberto y Juan son hermanos.	Robert and John are brothers.

e is used instead of *y* before words beginning with *i-* or *hi-*:

María e Isabel son hermanas.	Mary and Elizabeth are sisters.
Madre e hija.	Mother and daughter.

2. *o* "or"

Cinco o seis pesos.	Five or six pesos.
Voy con mi hermano o con mi hermana.	I'm going with my brother or (with) my sister.

u is used instead of *o* before words beginning with *e-* or *o-*:

Siete u ocho horas.	Seven or eight hours.
Cinco u ocho meses.	Five or eight months.

3. *pero* "but"

Quiero ir pero no sé cuando.	I want to go but I don't know when.
Quiero ir pero no puedo.	I want to go but I can't.

mas "but" is more formal and literary:

Pensé que vendría mas no pudo.	I thought he would come but he couldn't.

4. *sino* "but" is used instead of *pero* after a negative statement:

No es francés sino inglés.	He is not French but English.
No viene hoy sino mañana.	He is not coming today but tomorrow.

QUIZ 11

1. Inglés.	1. Five or six days.
2. Y.	2. He is not French but English.
3. Pero.	3. Seven or eight hours.
4. Hija.	4. English.
5. Hermano.	5. But.
6. Cinco o seis días.	6. Tomorrow.
7. Cuando.	7. Daughter.
8. No es francés sino inglés.	8. And.
9. Mañana.	9. When.
10. Siete u ocho horas.	10. Brother.

ANSWERS

1—4; 2—8; 3—5; 4—7; 5—10; 6—1; 7—9; 8—2; 9—6; 10—3.

LESSON 13

31. WHERE?

(Where?)

1. Where?

¿Dónde está?	Where is it?
Aquí.	Here.
Allí.	There.
A la derecha.	To the right.
A la izquierda.	To the left.
En la esquina.	On the corner.
Está en la calle de Alcalá.	It's on Alcala Street.
Está en la plaza de Santa Ana.	It's on Santa Ana Square.
Está en la avenida de Mayo.	It's on Mayo Avenue.
¿Por dónde?	Which way?
Por aquí.	This way.
Por allí.	That way.
¿Cómo se va allí?	How do you get there?
Vaya usted todo derecho.	Go straight ahead.
Doble usted a la derecha.	Turn to your right.
Doble usted a la izquierda.	Turn to your left.
¿Dónde es eso?	Where's the place you're talking about? ("Where is that?")
Es aquí.	It's here.
Es aquí mismo.	It's right here.

Es allí.	It's there.
Es más adelante.	It's farther.
Es un poco más allá.	It's a little farther.
¿Está lejos?	It is far?
¿Cuánto hay de aquí a allí?	How far is it from here to there.
Está cerca.	It's near.
No está muy lejos.	It's not too far.
¿Está lejos de aquí?	Is it far from here?
¿Dónde está el libro?	Where's the book?
Está aquí.	It's here.
Está aquí mismo.	It's right here.
Está ahí.	It's there (where you are).
Está allí.	It's over there (distant from both of us).
¿Dónde está usted?	Where are you?
Aquí estoy.	Here I am.
Aquí está.	Here he is.
Está aquí.	He's here.
Está ahí.	He's there.
Ahí va.	There he goes.
Está por ahí.	He's somewhere over there.
Póngalo aquí.	Put it here.
Póngalo ahí.	Put it there.
Espéreme aquí.	Wait for me here.
Espéreme ahí.	Wait for me there.
Venga usted acá.	Come here.
Acá viene.	Here he comes.
Vaya usted allá.	Go there.
Allá lejos.	Way over there.
Aquí cerca.	Around here. Near here.

LESSON 14

(Here and There)

Allá en Espanã.	Over there in Spain.
Aquí en América.	Here in America.
Allá dentro.	In there.
Allá fuera.	Out there.
¿Dónde vive?	Where does he live?
Vive allí.	He lives there.
Espero verle allí.	I expect to see him there.
Ella está allí.	She's there.
¿Es aquí donde vive Juan?	Does John live here? Is this where John lives?
Aquí es.	This is the place. It's here.
No es aquí.	It's not here.
Es allí.	It's there.
Vaya usted por aquí.	Go this way.
Vaya usted por allí.	Go that way.
Entre usted por aquí.	Come in this way.
Salga por allí.	Go out that way.

2. Here and There

Aquí "here" refers to something near the speaker:

Tengo aquí los libros.	I have the books here.

Ahí "there" refers to something near the person spoken to:

¿Qué tiene usted ahí?	What do you have there?
¿Está usted ahí?	Are you there?

Acá "here" expresses motion toward the speaker:

¡Venga usted acá!	Come here!

Allá "there" indicates motion away from the speaker:

Vaya usted allá.	Go there.
Mañana voy allá.	Tomorrow I'm going there.

Allí "there" refers to something remote from both:

Vienen de allí.	They've come from there.
Viví en Sur América por varios años. ¿Ha estado usted allí?	I (I've) lived in South America for several years. Have you ever been there?

Note: *Por aquí* means "this way" or "around here"; *por allí* means "that way" or "around there":

Vaya usted por aquí.	Go this way.

3. Near and Far

Cerca de aquí.	Near here.
Muy cerca.	Very near.
A dos pasos de aquí.	A few steps from here.
Cerca del pueblo.	Near the town.
Cerca del parque.	Near the park.
Al lado de la iglesia.	Next to the church.
¿Está lejos?	Is it far?
¿Está lejos de aquí?	Is it far from here?
Está muy lejos.	It's very far.
No está tan lejos.	It's not too far.
Está a dos cuadras de aquí.	It's two blocks from here.
Está a una milla de aquí.	It's a ("one") mile from here.

QUIZ 12

1. *Allá en España.*	1. I expect to see him there.
2. *Espéreme ahí.*	2. In there.
3. *Aquí.*	3. To the left.
4. *A la derecha.*	4. It's far.
5. *Allí.*	5. Here.
6. *Es aquí mismo.*	6. Wait for me here.
7. *Espero verle allí.*	7. Straight ahead.
8. *A la izquierda.*	8. To the right.
9. *Está lejos.*	9. There.
10. *Allá dentro.*	10. Out there.
11. *Está por ahí.*	11. Go that way.
12. *Está cerca.*	12. It's right here.
13. *Allá fuera.*	13. Over there in Spain.
14. *Vaya usted por allí.*	14. He's somewhere around here.
15. *Todo derecho.*	15. It's near.

ANSWERS

1—13; 2—6; 3—5; 4—8; 5—9; 6—12; 7—1; 8—3; 9—4; 10—2; 11—14; 12—15; 13—10; 14—11; 15—7.

32. I, YOU, HE

1. I, You, He

SINGULAR

yo	I
tú	you *(fam.)*
él	he
ella	she
ello	it
usted	you *(polite)*

(yo) hablo	I speak
(tú) hablas	you speak *(fam.)*
(él) habla	he speaks
(ella) habla	she speaks
(usted) habla	you speak

PLURAL

nosotros	we *(masc.)*
nosotras	we *(fem.)*
vosotros	you *(masc.)*
vosotras	you *(fem.)*
ellos	thcy *(masc.)*
ellas	they *(fem.)*
ustedes	you *(polite)*

(nosotros) hablamos	we speak
(nosotras) hablamos	we speak *(fem.)*
(vosotros) habláis	you speak
(vosotras) habláis	you spcak *(fem.)*
(ellos) hablan	they speak
(ellas) hablan	they speak *(fem.)*
(ustedes) hablan	you speak

The personal pronouns *yo*, *tú*, etc., are not ordinarily used; "I speak" is just *hablo*, "we speak" *hablamos*, etc. They are used only for emphasis or clearness.

2. It's Me (I)

Soy yo	It's me (I)
Eres tú	It's you
Es él	It's he
Es ella	It's she

Somos nosotros	It's us (we)
Sois vosotros	It's you *(masc.)*
Sois vosotras	It's you *(fem.)*
Son ellos	It's them (they) *(masc.)*
Son ellas	It's them (they) *(fem.)*

3. My, Your, His

mi amigo	my friend
un amigo mío	my friend (a friend of mine)

There are two forms for the pronouns *"my,"* *"your,"* *"his,"* etc.—one that precedes the noun (the commoner one) and one that follows (more emphatic):

PRECEDING THE NOUN

mi (pl. *mis)*	my
tu (pl. *tus)*	your *(fam.)*
su (pl. *sus)*	his, her, your *(polite)*
nuestro, -a (pl. *-os, -as)*	our
vuestro, -a (pl. *-os, -as)*	your *(fam.)*
su (pl. *sus)*	their, your *(polite)*

FOLLOWING THE NOUN

mío, mía (pl. *-os, -as)*	of mine
tuyo, -a (pl. *-os, -as)*	of yours
suyo, -a (pl. *-os, -as)*	of his, etc.
nuestro, -a (pl. *-os, -as)*	of ours
vuestro, -a (pl. *-os, -as)*	of yours *(fam.)*
suyo, -a (pl. *-os, -as)*	of yours

LESSON 15

(Useful Word Forms)

The pronoun is often repeated for clearness or emphasis:

Yo lo tengo.	I have it.
¿Qué le pasa a usted?	What's the matter with you?
Le doy el libro.	I give him (her, you) the book.
Le doy el libro a él.	I give him the book.

Le doy el libro a ella.	I give her the book.
Le doy el libro a usted.	I give you the book.
Me gusta el libro.	I like the book.
A mí me gusta el libro.	*I* like the book *(even if you don't)*.

Study the following examples:

SINGULAR

mi amigo	my friend
tu amigo	your friend
su amigo	his, her, your friend
nuestro amigo	our friend
nuestra amiga	our friend
vuestro amigo	your friend
vuestra amiga	your friend
su amigo	their friend, your friend

PLURAL

mis amigos	my friends
tus amigos	your friends
sus amigos	his, her, your friends
nuestros amigos	our friends
nuestras amigas	our friends
vuestros amigos	your friends
vuestras amigas	your friends
sus amigos	their friends, your friends

SINGULAR

mi sombrero	my hat
tu vestido	your dress
su vestido	her dress
nuestro amigo	our friend
nuestra madre	our mother
vuestro hijo	your son
vuestra hija	your daughter

PLURAL

mis sombreros	my hats
tus vestidos	your dresses
sus vestidos	her dresses
nuestros amigos	our friends
nuestras madres	our mothers
vuestros hijos	your sons
vuestras hijas	your daughters

Other Examples:

MASCULINE SINGULAR

¿Dónde está mi hermano?	Where is my brother?
¿Dónde está tu hermano?	Where is your brother?
¿Dónde está su hermano?	Where is his (her, your) brother?
¿Dónde está nuestro hermano?	Where is our brother?
¿Dónde está vuestro hermano?	Where is your brother?
¿Dónde está su hermano?	Where is their brother?

FEMININE SINGULAR

¿Dónde está mi hermana?	Where is my sister?
¿Dónde está tu hermana?	Where is your sister?
¿Dónde está su hermana?	Where is his (her, your) sister?
¿Dónde está nuestra hermana?	Where is our sister?
¿Dónde está vuestra hermana?	Where is your sister?
¿Dónde está su hermana?	Where is their sister?

MASCULINE PLURAL

¿Dónde están mis libros?	Where are my books?
¿Dónde están tus libros?	Where are your books?
¿Dónde están sus libros?	Where are his (her, your) books?

¿Dónde están nuestros libros?	Where are our books?
¿Dónde están vuestros libros?	Where are your books?
¿Dónde están sus libros?	Where are their books?

FEMININE PLURAL

¿Dónde están mis cartas?	Where are my letters?
¿Dónde están tus cartas?	Where are your letters?
¿Dónde están sus cartas?	Where are his (her, your) letters?
¿Dónde están nuestras cartas?	Where are our letters?
¿Dónde están vuestras cartas?	Where are your letters?
¿Dónde están sus cartas?	Where are their letters?

4. It's Mine

There are two forms—one with *el* and one without:

a.

Es mío.	It's mine.
Es tuyo.	It's yours.
Es suyo.	It's his (hers, yours).
Es nuestro.	It's ours.
Es vuestro.	It's yours.
Es suyo.	It's theirs.

b.

Es el mío.	It's mine.
Es el tuyo.	It's yours.
Es el suyo.	It's his (hers, yours).
Es el nuestro.	It's ours.
Es el vuestro.	It's yours.
Es el suyo.	It's theirs.

The form with *el* means something like "It's the one which belongs to me."

Other Examples:

Mis amigos y los tuyos.	My friends and yours.
Su libro es mejor que el nuestro.	His book is better than ours.
¿De quién es la carta?—Suya.	Whose letter is this?—His.

Notice the form of the pronoun when it comes after a preposition:

SINGULAR

para mí	for me
por ti	for your sake
con él	with him
a ella	to her
para usted	for you

PLURAL

sin nosotros	without us
con vosotros	with you
para ellos	for them *(masc.)*
para ellas	for them *(fem.)*
de ustedes	of you

5. He Saw Me

Me vió a mí.	He (she) saw me.
Te vió a ti.	He (she) saw you.
Le ví a usted.	I saw you.
Le ví a él.	I saw him.
La ví a ella.	I saw her.

Nos vieron a nosotros.	They saw us.
Les vimos a ellos.	We saw them *(masc.)*
Las vimos a ellas.	We saw them *(fem.)*

6. About Me

Hablo de tí.	I'm speaking about you.
Hablas de mí.	You *(fam.)* are speaking about me.

Habla de él.	He (she) is speaking about him.
Habla de ella.	He (she) is speaking about her.
Hablamos de ustedes.	We are speaking about you *(pl.)*.
Habláis de nosotras.	You are speaking about us *(fem.)*.
Hablan de ellos.	They are speaking about them *(masc.)*.
Hablan de ellas.	They are speaking about them *(fem.)*.

7. To Me

Me lo dijo a mí.	He (she) told it to me.
Te lo dijo a tí.	He (she) told it to you.
Se lo dijo a él.	He (she) told it to him.
Se lo dijo a ella.	He (she) told it to her.
Nos lo dijo a nosotros.	He (she) told it to us.
Os lo dijo a vosotros.	He (she) told it to you.
Se lo dijo a ellos.	He (she) told it to them.

8. He Gave It to Me

Me lo dió.	He gave it to me.
Te lo dió.	He gave it to you.
Se lo dió.	He gave it to you.
Nos lo dió.	He gave it to us.
Se lo dió.	He gave it to them.

9. I'm Speaking to You

Le hablo.	I'm speaking to you.
Te habla.	He (she) is speaking to you.
Le habla.	He (she) is speaking to you *(polite)*.

10. He Told Me

Me dijo.	He (she) told me.
Te dijo.	He (she) told you.
Le dijo.	He (she) told you.
Nos dijo.	He (she) told us.
Os dijo.	He (she) told you.
Les dijo.	He (she) told them.

11. Myself, Yourself

Yo me lavo.	I wash myself.
Tú te lavas.	You wash yourself.
El se lava.	He washes himself.
Ella se lava.	She washes herself.
Usted se lava.	You wash yourself.
Nosotros nos lavamos.	We wash ourselves.
Vosotros os laváis.	You wash yourselves.
Ellos se lavan.	They wash themselves.

Other Examples:

¿Cómo se llama usted?	What's your name? ("What do you call yourself?")
Nos vemos en el espejo.	We see ourselves in the mirror.
Se escriben.	They write to one another.

Notice the forms for "myself," "yourself," etc.: *me, te, se,* etc. Verbs which take these "reflexive pronouns" are called "reflexive" verbs. Many verbs are reflexive in Spanish which are not in English:

Me divierto.	I'm having a good time.
Me engaño.	I'm mistaken.
Me siento.	I sit down. I'm sitting down.

Me levanto.	I get up. I'm getting up (standing up).
Me voy.	I'm going away. I'm leaving.
Se me ocurre.	I have an idea. It occurs to me.
Se me olvida.	I forget.
Se me figura.	I imagine.

In Spanish you don't say "I'm washing my hands" but "I'm washing the hands"; not "Take your hat off" but "Take off the hat":

Me lavo las manos.	I'm washing my hands.
Quítese el sombrero.	Take your hat off.
Se ha roto el brazo.	He broke (has broken) his arm.
Se ha cortado un dedo.	She's cut her finger.
Me he lastimado la mano.	I've hurt my hand.
Me duele la cabeza.	I have a headache.
Me duele el estómago.	I have a stomach-ache.
Estoy perdiendo la paciencia.	I'm losing my patience.

The reflexive forms are often used where we would use the passive in English:

Aquí se habla español.	Spanish spoken here.
Se abren las puertas a las ocho.	The doors are opened at eight.

The reflexive forms are also often used to translate our "one," "they," "people," etc.

Se dice que . . .	It's said that . . . People say that . . . They say that . . .
Se come bien aquí.	The food's good here. ("One eats well here.")

QUIZ 13

1. *Me siento.*	1. I get up.
2. *Se me ocurre.*	2. I'm leaving.
3. *Me divierto.*	3. I forget.
4. *Se me figura.*	4. I'm mistaken.
5. *Me levanto.*	5. I wash myself.
6. *Me lavo.*	6. I'm having a good time.
7. *Me engaño.*	7. They write to one another.
8. *Se escriben.*	8. I imagine.
9. *Se me olvida.*	9. It occurs to me.
10. *Me voy.*	10. I sit down.

ANSWERS

1—10; 2—9; 3—6; 4—8; 5—1; 6—5; 7—4; 8—7; 9—3; 10—2.

12. It and Them

SINGULAR			PLURAL	
Masculine	*lo*	it	*los*	them
Feminine	*la*	it	*las*	them

¿Tiene usted el dinero?	Do you have the money?
Sí, lo tengo.	Yes, I have it.
¿Tiene usted la carta?	Do you have the letter?
Sí, la tengo.	Yes, I have it.
¿Vió usted a Juan y a Pedro?	Did you see John and Peter?
Sí, los ví.	Yes, I saw them.
¿Vió usted a María y a Carmen?	Did you see Mary and Carmen?
Sí, las ví.	Yes, I saw them.

Notice that the pronoun is masculine if the word it refers to is masculine, plural if the word it refers to is plural, etc.

Lo is used for "it" when the reference is to an idea or a whole expression:

Lo comprendo.	I understand it.

Notice that these forms usually come immediately before the verb. In case of the infinitive ("to understand," etc.) they follow:

Quiere comprenderlo.	He's trying to understand it.

Notice the use of *le, la, les* and *las* in the *usted* form—that is, the form you use in speaking to people whom you don't know very well or with whom your relationship is rather formal.

¡Mucho gusto en (de) verle!	Glad to see you! *(speaking to a man)*
¡Mucho gusto en (de) verla!	Glad to see you! *(speaking to a woman)*
¡Mucho gusto en (de) verles!	Glad to see you! *(speaking to several men or a group of men and women)*
¡Mucho gusto en (de) verlas!	Glad to see you! *(speaking to several women)*

REVIEW QUIZ 3

1. *Es* _____ (she).
   a. *él*
   b. *ella*
   c. *yo*

2. *Somos* _____ (us).
   a. *ellos*
   b. *tú*
   c. *nosotros*

3. *Le doy el libro a* _____ (him).
   a. *él*
   b. *usted*
   c. *lo*

4. _____ (her) *vestido.*
   a. *su*
   b. *mi*
   c. *nuestro*

5. _____ (our) *cartas.*
   a. *nuestro*
   b. *nuestras*
   c. *tuyo*

6. *¿Dónde están* _____ (my) *libros?*
   a. *tus*
   b. *mis*
   c. *nuestra*

7. *Su libro es mejor que el* _____ (ours).
   a. *tuyos*
   b. *nuestro*
   c. *su*

8. *Hablamos de* _____ (him).
   a. *tí*
   b. *ellos*
   c. *él*

9. _____ (us) *lo dió.*
   a. *se*
   b. *nos*
   c. *nosotros*

10. ¿Cómo se _____ (call) usted?
    a. lavo
    b. llama
    c. vemos

11. Nosotros nos _____ (wash).
    a. lava
    b. laváis
    c. lavamos

12. Me _____ (mistaken).
    a. engaño
    b. levanto
    c. ocurre

13. Me _____ (sit down).
    a. voy
    b. figure
    c. siento

14. Me he _____ (hurt) la mano.
    a. roto
    b. lavo
    c. lastimado

15. Me _____ (leaving, going away).
    a. voy
    b. vemos
    c. llama

ANSWERS

1 b.; 2 c.; 3 a.; 4 a.; 5 b.; 6 b.; 7 b.; 8 c.; 9 b.; 10 b.;
11 c.; 12 a.; 13 c.; 14 c.; 15 a.

LESSON 16

33. A FEW SHORT PHRASES

(Useful Phrases)

¡Cuidado!	Watch out!
¡Tenga cuidado!	Be careful! Watch out!
¡Dése prisa!	Fast! Hurry up!
¡Vaya de prisa!	Go fast!
Más de prisa.	Faster.
No tan de prisa.	No so fast.
No muy de prisa.	Not very fast.
Menos de prisa.	Slower.
Más despacio.	Slower.
¡Voy!	I'm coming.
Voy corriendo.	I'm coming right away.
Voy en seguida.	I'm coming right away.
Dése usted prisa.	Hurry up.
No se dé usted prisa.	Don't hurry.
Tengo prisa.	I'm in a hurry.
No tengo prisa.	I'm not in a hurry.
¡Un momento!	Just a minute! In a minute!
¡Al instante!	Right away!
¡Venga en seguida!	Come right away!
Pronto.	Soon.
Immediatamente.	Immediately.
Más pronto.	Sooner.
Más tarde.	Later.

QUIZ 14

1. *¡Cuidado!*	1. Slower.
2. *Tengo prisa.*	2. Right away.
3. *¡Un momento!*	3. Come right away.
4. *Pronto.*	4. I'm coming.
5. *Inmediatemente.*	5. Watch out!
6. *Más tarde.*	6. Later.
7. *Más despacio.*	7. I'm in a hurry.
8. *¡Voy!*	8. Just a minute! In a minute!
9. *Venga en seguida.*	9. Immediately.
10. *Al instante.*	10. Soon.

ANSWERS

1—5; 2—7; 3—8; 4—10; 5—9; 6—6; 7—1; 8—4; 9—3; 10—2.

34. MAY I ASK?

¿Me permite que le haga una pregunta?	May I ask you a question?
¿Permítame que le pregunte . . . ?	May I ask(you) . . . ?
¿Puede decirme?	Can you tell me?
¿Podría decirme?	Could you tell me?
¿Quiere decirme?	Will you tell me?
Sírvase decirme.	Could you please tell me?
Haga el favor de decirme.	Could you please tell me?
¿Qué quiere usted decir?	What do you mean?
Quiero decir que . . .	I mean that . . .
¿Qué quiere decir eso?	What does that mean?
Esto quiere decir . . .	This means . . .

35. NUMBERS

1. One, Two, Three

uno	one
dos	two
tres	three
cuatro	four
cinco	five
seis	six
siete	seven
ocho	eight
nueve	nine
diez	ten
once	eleven
doce	twelve
trece	thirteen
catorce	fourteen
quince	fifteen
dieciséis	sixteen
diecisiete	seventeen
dieciocho	eighteen
diecinueve	nineteen
veinte	twenty
veinte (veinte y uno)	twenty-one
veintidós (veinte y dos)	twenty-two

LESSON 17

(Numbers)

veintitrés (veinte y tres)	twenty-three
trienta	thirty
treintiuno (treinta y uno)	thirty-one
treintidós (treinta y dos)	thirty-two

treintitrés (treinta y tres)	thirty-three
cuarenta	forty
cuarentiuno (cuarenta y uno)	forty-one
cuarentidós (cuarenta y dos)	forty-two
cuarentitrés (cuarenta y tres)	forty-three
cincuenta	fifty
cincuentiuno (cincuenta y uno)	fifty-one
cincuentidós (cincuenta y dos)	fifty-two
cincuentitrés (cincuenta y tres)	fifty-three
sesenta	sixty
sesentiuno (sesenta y uno)	sixty-one
sesentidós (sesenta y dos)	sixty-two
sesentitrés (sesenta y tres)	sixty-three
setenta	seventy
setentiuno (setenta y uno)	seventy-one
setendidós (setenta y dos)	seventy-two
setentitrés (setenta y tres)	seventy-three
ochenta	eighty
ochentiuno (ochenta y uno)	eighty-one

ochentidós (ochenta y dos)	eighty-two
ochentitrés (ochenta y tres)	eighty-three
noventa	ninety
noventiuno (noventa y uno)	ninety-one
noventidós (noventa y dos)	ninety-two
noventitrés (noventa y tres)	ninety-three
cien	hundred
ciento uno	a hundred and one
ciento dos	a hundred and two
ciento tres	a hundred and three
mil	thousand
mil uno	a thousand and one
mil dos	a thousand and two
mil tres	a thousand and three

2. Some More Numbers

120 *ciento veinte*
122 *ciento veintidós (ciento veinte y dos)*
130 *ciento treinta*
140 *ciento cuarenta*
150 *ciento cincuenta*
160 *ciento sesenta*
170 *ciento setenta*
171 *ciento setentiuno (ciento setenta y uno)*
178 *ciento setentiocho (ciento setenta y ocho)*
180 *ciento ochenta*
182 *ciento ochentidós (ciento ochenta y dos)*
190 *ciento noventa*

198 *ciento noventiocho (ciento noventa y ocho)*

199 *ciento noventinueve (ciento noventa y nueve)*

200 *doscientos*

324 *trescientos veinticuatro (trescientos veinte y cuatro)*

875 *ochocientos setenticinco (ochocientos setenta y cinco)*

LESSON 18

(How Much?)

3. First, Second, Third

primero	first
segundo	second
tercero	third
cuarto	fourth
quinto	fifth
sexto	sixth
séptimo	seventh
octavo	eighth
noveno	ninth
décimo	tenth

4. Two and Two

Dos y dos son cuatro.	Two and two are four.
Dos más dos son cuatro.	Two and two are four.
Cuatro más dos son seis.	Four and two are six.
Diez menos dos son ocho.	Ten minus two is eight.

QUIZ 15

1.	mil	1.	1002
2.	once	2.	32
3.	cien	3.	102
4.	diecisiete	4.	324
5.	treinta	5.	11
6.	veinte	6.	1000
7.	sesenta	7.	60
8.	trescientos veinticuatro	8.	71
9.	treintidós	9.	17
10.	ciento dos	10.	875
11.	ochocientos setenticinco	11.	83
12.	setentiuno	12.	93
13.	mil dos	13.	20
14.	noventitrés	14.	30
15.	ochentitrés	15.	100

ANSWERS

1—6; 2—5; 3—15; 4—9; 5—14; 6—13; 7—7; 8—4;
9—2; 10—3; 11—10; 12—8; 13—1; 14—12; 15—11.

36. HOW MUCH?

¿Cuánto cuesta esto?	How much does this cost?
Cuesta cuarenta centavos.	It costs forty cents.
¿A cómo se vende la libra de café?	How much is a pound of coffee?
Se vende a treinta centavos la libra.	It costs thirty cents a pound.

37. IT COSTS...

Cuesta...	It costs...
Este libro cuesta tres pesos.	This book costs three pesos.

Compró un coche por dos mil dólares.	He bought a car for two thousand dollars.
El viaje en tren de Colón a Panamá cuesta veinte pesos.	The trip by train from Colon to Panama costs twenty pesos.
He ahorrado veintidós dólares para comprarme un vestido.	I've saved twenty-two dollars to buy clothing.
En el mes de junio hizo cinco mil ochocientos treinticuatro pesos.	He made 5834 pesos in the month of June.
Se vende solamente por libras, y cuesta tres pesos la libra.	It's sold only by the pound and costs three pesos a pound.

38. MY ADDRESS IS . . .

Yo vivo en el doscientos cincuenta de la calle Rivadavia.	I live at 250 Rivadavia Street.
Ella vive en el trescientos del Paseo de García.	She lives at 300 Paseo de García.
La tienda queda en el trescientos veintiséis de la Avenida de Mayo.	The store is at 326 Mayo Avenue.
Se trasladaron a la Plaza de Colón, número novecientos veintiuno.	They moved to 921 Columbus Plaza.

39. MY TELEPHONE NUMBER IS . . .

El número de mi teléfono es tres dos ocho ocho.	My telephone number is 3288.

El número de su teléfono es cuatro cero ocho seis cero.	Their telephone number is: 4-0860.
No se le olvide el número de mi teléfono; es seis cinco cero seis.	Don't forget my telephone number: 6506.
Central, tenga la bondad de darme el tres seis nueve dos.	Operator, may I have ("please give me") 3692?
El número seis ocho siete cinco no contesta.	Number 6875 doesn't answer.

40. THE NUMBER IS . . .

El número es . . .	The number is . . .
Mi número es . . .	My number is . . .
El número de mi cuarto es el treinta.	My room number is 30.
Vivo en cuarto número treinta.	I live in room 30.
El número de mi casa es el mil trescientos veintidós.	My address ("house number") is 1322.
Vivo en el quinto piso, del trescientos treintidós de la Quinta Avenida.	I live at 332 Fifth Avenue, fifth floor.

LESSON 19

41. WHAT'S TODAY?

(What's the Date?)

¿Qué dia de la semana es hoy?	What's today? ("What day of the week is today?")
Es el lunes.	Monday.

The following expressions all mean "What's the date?":

¿A cómo estamos?	("At how are we?")
¿A cómo estamos hoy?	("At how are we today?")
¿A cuántos estamos?	("At how many are we?")
¿En qué fecha estamos?	("In what date are we?")
Estamos a veinte.	It's the 20th. ("We're at the 20th.")
El primero de mayo.	The 1st of May.
El once de abril.	The 11th of April.
El cuatro de julio.	The 4th of July.
El quince de septiembre.	The 15th of September.
El veintiuno de junio	The 21st of June.
El veinticinco de diciembre.	The 25th of December.
El diecisiete de noviembre.	The 17th of November.
El trece de febrero.	The 13th of February.
El veintiocho de agosto.	The 28th of August.

42. SOME DATES

La América fué descubierta en mil cuatrocientos noventidós.	America was discovered in 1492.
Don Quijote fué publicado en mil seiscientos cinco.	"Don Quixote" was published in 1605.

Shakespeare y Cervantes murieron en mil seiscientos dieciséis.	Shakespeare and Cervantes both died in 1616.
Su padre murió en mil novecientos veinticuatro.	His father died in 1924.
Estuvimos allí en mil novecientos treintidós o mil novecientos treintitrés.	We were there in 1932 or 1933.
¿Qué sucedió en mil novecientos cuarentiuno?	What happened in 1941?
El presidente Roosevelt murió en mil novecientos cuarenticinco.	President Roosevelt died in 1945.

QUIZ 16

1. *Es el lunes.*	1. The 25th of June.
2. *¿A cuántos estamos?*	2. The 28th of February.
3. *El primero de julio.*	3. The 13th of August.
4. *¿En qué fecha estamos?*	4. 1605.
5. *El once de abril.*	5. It's Monday.
6. *El veintiocho de febrero.*	6. What day of the month is it?
7. *El veinticinco de junio.*	7. Date.
8. *Mil seiscientos cinco.*	8. The first of July.
9. *El trece de agosto.*	9. The 11th of April.
10. *Fecha.*	10. What's the date?

ANSWERS

1—5; 2—6; 3—8; 4—10; 5—9; 6—2; 7—1; 8—4; 9—3; 10—7.

43. WHAT TIME IS IT?

¿Qué hora es?	What time is it?
Es la una.	1:00.
Es la una y cinco.	1:05.
Es la una y diez.	1:10.
Es la una y quince.	1:15.
Es la una y cuarto.	1:15.
Es la una y media.	1:30.
Es la una y cincuenta.	1:50.
Faltan diez para las dos.	1:50.("ten minutes to two").
Son las dos.	2:00.
Son las tres.	3:00.
Son las cuatro.	4:00.
Son las cinco.	5:00.
Son las seis.	6:00.
Son las siete.	7:00.
Son las ocho.	8:00.
Son las nueve.	9:00.
Son las diez.	10:00.
Son las once.	11:00.
Son las doce.	12:00 noon. It's noon.
Es la mediodía.	12:00. It's noon.
Es la medianoche.	12:00 midnight. It's midnight.
minuto.	minute.
hora.	hour.
¿A qué hora?	(At) what time?
¿Tiene usted la bondad de decirme la hora?	Can you please tell me the time?
¿Qué hora tiene usted?	What time do you have?
Mi reloj marca las cinco.	It's 5 o'clock by my watch. ("My watch marks 5 o'clock.")

LESSON 20

(What Time Is It?)

Son las tres y diez.	It's 3:10.
Son las seis y media.	It's 6:30.
Son las dos menos cuarto.	It's a quarter to 2.
No son todavía las cuatro.	It's not four yet.
¿A qué hora sale el tren?	What time does the train leave?
A las nueve en punto.	At 9 o'clock sharp.
Cerca de las nueve.	About 9 o'clock.
Hacia las nueve.	Around 9 o'clock.
Son las diez de la mañana.	It's 10 a.m.
A las tres menos veinte del día.	At 2:40 p.m. ("twenty minutes to three").
A las seis de la tarde.	At 6 p.m.
A las seis de la noche.	

Notice that when you want to specify "a.m." or "p.m." in Spanish you add *de la mañana*, *del día* or *de la noche (de la tarde)*.

44. IT'S TIME

Es hora.	It's time.
Es hora de hacerlo.	It's time to do it.
Es hora de partir.[1]	It's time to leave.
Es hora de irnos a casa.	It's time for us to go home.
Tengo mucho tiempo.	I have a lot of time.
No tengo tiempo.	I haven't any time.
Está perdiendo su tiempo.	He's wasting his time.
Viene de vez en cuando.	He comes from time to time.

[1] Or you might choose to say: *Es hora de salir.*

QUIZ 17

1. Es hora de hacerlo.	1. He comes from time to time.
2. ¿Qué hora es?	2. It's 9:00.
3. Es la una.	3. At what time?
4. Son las tres.	4. It's time to do it.
5. Son las nueve.	5. It's 2:00.
6. Es la medianoche.	6. It's 1:00.
7. ¿A qué hora?	7. I haven't any time.
8. No tengo tiempo.	8. It's 2:40 p.m. ("twenty minutes to 3").
9. Es la una y cuarto.	9. It's noon.
10. Son las cuatro.	10. It's 3:00.
11. Son las dos.	11. It's 1:05.
12. Viene de vez en cuando.	12. It's 4:00.
13. Es el mediodía.	13. What time is it?
14. Es la una y cinco.	14. It's 1:15.
15. Son las tres menos veinte del día.	15. It's midnight.

ANSWERS

1—4; 2—13; 3—6; 4—10; 5—2; 6—15; 7—3; 8—7; 9—14; 10—12; 11—5; 12—1; 13—9; 14—11; 15—8.

45. PAST, PRESENT AND FUTURE

PASADO	PRESENTE	FUTURO
ayer	**hoy**	**mañana**
yesterday	today	tomorrow
ayer por la mañana	**esta mañana**	**mañana por la mañana**
yesterday morning	this morning	tomorrow morning

PASADO	PRESENTE	FUTURO
ayer por la tarde last evening	**esta tarde** this evening	**mañana por la tarde** tomorrow evening
anoche last night	**esta noche** tonight	**mañana por la noche** tomorrow night

46. MORNING, NOON AND NIGHT

Esta mañana.	This morning.
Ayer por la mañana.	Yesterday morning.
Mañana por la mañana.	Tomorrow morning.
Hoy a mediodía.	This noon.
Ayer a mediodía.	Yesterday noon.
Mañana a mediodía.	Tomorrow noon.
Esta tarde.	This evening.
Ayer por la tarde.	Yesterday evening.
Mañana por la tarde.	Tomorrow evening.
Esta noche.	Tonight.
Anoche.	Last night.
Mañana por la noche.	Tomorrow night.

LESSON 21

(Past, Present and Future)

Esta semana.	This week.
La semana pasada.	Last week.
La semana entrante.	Next week.
Dentro de dos semanas.	In two weeks.
Hace dos semanas.	Two weeks ago.

La semana antepasada.	The week before last.
Este mes.	This month.
El mes pasado.	Last month.
El mes que viene.	Next month ("the month that's coming").
El mes entrante.	Next month.
Dentro de dos meses.	In two months.
Hace dos meses.	Two months ago.
El mes antepasado.	The month before last.
Este año.	This year.
El año pasado.	Last year.
El año entrante.	Next year.
El año que viene.	Next year.
Dentro de dos años.	In two years.
El año después del que viene.	The year after next.
Hace dos años.	Two years ago.
El año antepasado.	The year before last.
¿Cuánto tiempo hace?	How long ago?
Hace un momento.	A moment ago ("it makes a minute").
Hace mucho tiempo.	A long time ago ("it makes much time").
Ahora.	Now.
Ahora mismo.	This very moment.
Por ahora.	For the time being.
En este momento.	At this moment.
De momento.	For the time being.
De un momento a otro.	At any moment.
Dentro de un momento.	In a short time.
Dentro de poco.	In a little while.
A ratos.	From time to time.
¿Cuántas veces?	How many times?
Una vez.	Once.
Cada vez.	Each time.

Dos veces.	Twice.
Rara vez.	Very seldom. Not often.
Muchas veces.	Very often.
A veces.	Sometimes.
Alguna que otra vez.	Once in a while.
De vez en cuando.	Now and then. From time to time.
Por la mañana temprano.	Early in the morning.
Al anochecer.	In the evening ("at nightfall").
Al otro día.	On the following day.
Al día siguiente.	On the following day.
De hoy en quince días.	Two weeks from today.
De hoy en ocho días.	A week from today.
De mañana en ocho días.	A week from tomorrow.
Dentro de una semana.	In a week.
El miércoles de la semana que viene.	Next Wednesday.
El lunes de la semana pasada.	Monday a week ago.
El cinco del corriente.	The fifth of this month.
El cinco del mes pasado.	The fifth of last month.
A principios de marzo.	At the beginning of March.
A fin de mes.	At the end of the month.
A principios de año.	In the early part of the year.
A fines de año.	Towards the end of the year.
Sucedió hace ocho años.	It happened eight years ago.

QUIZ 18

1. *Ayer por la mañana.*	1. Last year.
2. *Esta tarde.*	2. Last night.
3. *Mañana por la tarde.*	3. Today at noon.
4. *Anoche.*	4. Now.
5. *El mes que viene.*	5. In two weeks.
6. *Ahora.*	6. In a little while.
7. *La semana pasada.*	7. Yesterday morning.
8. *El año pasado.*	8. From time to time.
9. *Hoy a mediodía.*	9. It happened eight years ago.
10. *Dentro de poco.*	10. This afternoon.
11. *Esta semana.*	11. Sometimes.
12. *Sucedió hace ocho años.*	12. Within a week.
13. *A fines de año.*	13. Tomorrow afternoon.
14. *Hace dos meses.*	14. Next month.
15. *A fines de mes.*	15. Last week.
16. *Dentro de una semana.*	16. Each time.
17. *A ratos.*	17. About the end of the month.
18. *A veces.*	18. Towards the end of the year.
19. *Dentro de dos semanas.*	19. This week.
20. *Cada vez.*	20. Two months ago.

ANSWERS

1—7; 2—10; 3—13; 4—2; 5—14; 6—4; 7—15; 8—1; 9—3; 10—6; 11—19; 12—9; 13—18; 14—20; 15—17; 16—12; 17—8; 18—11; 19—5; 20—16.

REVIEW QUIZ 4

1. *Compró un coche por* _____ (four thousand)
   dólares.
   a. *tres mil*
   b. *cuatrocientos*
   c. *cuatro mil*

2. *El número de su teléfono es* _____ (4-0860).
   a. *seis, cinco, cero, seis, nueve*
   b. *tres, seis, nueve, dos, cero*
   c. *cuatro, cero, ocho, seis, cero*

3. *¿En qué* _____ (date) *estamos?*
   a. *día*
   b. *mes*
   c. *fecha*

4. *¿A cómo estamos* _____ (today)*?*
   a. *mes*
   b. *hoy*
   c. *cómo*

5. *El* _____ (17) *de diciembre.*
   a. *diecisiete*
   b. *veintisiete*
   c. *quince*

6. *Es la* _____ (1:10).
   a. *una y cinco*
   b. *una y diez*
   c. *una y cuarto*

7. *Son las* _____ (7:00).
   a. *siete*
   b. *nueve*
   c. *seis*

8. *Es el* _____ (12:00 noon).
   a. *medianoche*
   b. *mediodía*
   c. *once*

9. *A las* _____ (2:40).
   a. *falta un cuarto para las cuatro*
   b. *tres menos veinte*
   c. *una y cuarenticinco*

10. _____ (yesterday) *por la mañana.*
    a. *hoy*
    b. *ayer*
    c. *esta*

11. *La* _____ (week) *pasada.*
    a. *semana*
    b. *noche*
    c. *mañana*

12. *Dentro de dos* _____ (months).
    a. *semana*
    b. *día*
    c. *meses*

13. *Hace dos* _____ (years).
    a. *meses*
    b. *años*
    c. *días*

14. *El* _____ (Wednesday) *de la semana que viene.*
    a. *lunes*
    b. *viernes*
    c. *miércoles*

15. A _____ (end) *del año.*
  a. fines
  b. principios
  c. primeros

ANSWERS

1 c.; 2 c.; 3 c.; 4 b.; 5 a.; 6 b.; 7 a.; 8 b.; 9 b.; 10 b.;
11 a.; 12 c.; 13 b.; 14 c.; 15 a.

LESSON 22

47. NO

(Useful Word Groups I)

The word for "not"—*no*—comes before the verb:

No veo.	I don't see.
Usted no ve.	You don't see.

There are two forms for "nothing," "never," "nobody," etc.—one with and one without *no:*

No veo nada.	I see nothing. I don't see anything.
No voy nunca.	I never go.
No viene nadie.	No one is coming. Nobody comes.

Or—

Nada veo.	I see nothing. I don't see anything.
Nunca voy.	I never go.
Nadie viene.	No one is coming. Nobody comes.

Sí, señor.	Yes, sir.
No, señor.	No, sir.
Dice que sí.	He says yes.
Dice que no.	He says no.
Creo que sí.	I think so.
No está bien.	It's not good.
No está mal.	It's not bad.
No es eso.	It's not that.
No está aqui.	He's not here.
Aquí está.	It's here.
No es mucho.	It's not too much.
No es suficiente.	It's not enough.
Es bastante.	It's enough.
No tan de prisa.	Not so fast.
No tan a menudo.	Not so often.
No es nada.	It's nothing.
Eso no es nada.	That's nothing.
No es gran cosa.	It's not very important.
No tengo tiempo.	I have no time.
No sé cómo ni cuándo.	I don't know how or when.
No sé dónde.	I don't know where.
No sé nada.	I don't know anything.
No sé nada de eso.	I know nothing about it.
No quiero nada.	I don't want anything.
Nada quiero.	I don't want anything.
No importa.	It doesn't matter. It's not important.
No me importa.	I don't care. It makes no difference to me.
No me importa nada.	I don't care at all. It doesn't make the slightest difference to me.
No lo diga.	Don't say it.

No tengo nada que decir.	I've nothing to say.
Nunca lo diré.	I'll never say it.
No ha pasado nada.	Nothing happened.
No tengo nada que hacer.	I have nothing to do.
Nunca le veo.	I never see him.
Nunca le he visto.	I've never seen him before.
Jamás le he visto.	I've never seen him before.
Nunca viene.	He never comes.
Jamás ha venido.	He has never come.
Nunca voy.	I never go.
Jamás iré.	I'll never go.

LESSON 23

(Useful Word Groups II)

Ni.
Nor.

No he dicho ni una palabra.
I haven't said a word.

Ni . . . ni.
Neither . . . nor.

Ni más ni menos.
Just so ("neither more nor less.").

Ni el uno ni el otro.
Neither the one nor the other.

Ni esto ni aquello.
Neither this nor that.

Ni tanto ni tan poco.
Neither too much nor too little.

No es bueno ni malo.
It's so, so. It's not too good and not too bad.

No puedo ni quiero ir.
I can't go and I don't want to.

No tengo ni tiempo ni dinero.
I have neither the time nor the money.

No sabe leer ni escribir.
He can neither read nor write.

No tengo cigarrillos ni fósforos.
I haven't any cigarettes or matches.

48. USEFUL WORD GROUPS II

1. Isn't It, etc.

¿Verdad?
Is it?

¿No es verdad?
Isn't it?

El español es fácil, ¿no es verdad?
Spanish is easy, isn't it?

La gente aquí es muy simpática, ¿no es verdad?
The people here are very nice, aren't they?

Usted no tiene lápiz, ¿verdad?
You don't have a pencil, do you?

Usted conoce este lugar, ¿no es verdad?
You know this place, don't you?

Usted conoce al Sr. Díaz[1], ¿no es verdad?
You know Mr. Diaz, don't you?

---

[1]*Sr.* is the abbreviation for *señor.*

Usted tiene cuchara y servilleta, ¿no es verdad?
You have a spoon and a napkin, haven't you?

Usted no tiene mucho de estar aquí, ¿verdad?
You haven't been here very long, have you?

Vendrá usted, ¿no es verdad?
You'll come, won't you?

Hace frío, ¿no es verdad?
It's cold, isn't it?

¡Qué mono! ¿Verdad?
Isn't it cute? It's cute, isn't it?

Está bien, ¿verdad?
It's all right, isn't it?

2. Some, Any, A Few
¿Tiene Ud. dinero?
Do you have any money?

Sí, tengo algo.
Yes, I have some.

No, no tengo nada.
No, I don't have any.

¿Tiene algún dinero?
Does he have any money?

Algún dinero tiene.
He has some.

No tiene nada.
He doesn't have any.

¿Le queda a usted algún dinero?
Do you have money left? ("Does any money
  remain to you?")

Algo me queda.
I have some left. ("Some remains to me.")

¿Cuántos libros tiene?
How many books do you have?

Tengo unos pocos.
I have a few.

¿Quiere Ud. algunas frutas?
Do you want some fruit?

Déme usted unas cuantas.
Give me a few.

QUIZ 19

1. *No veo.*	1. Neither this nor that.
2. *No es nada.*	2. I have no time.
3. *Nunca lo diré.*	3. Don't tell it to him.
4. *No voy nunca.*	4. Nothing happened.
5. *No ve a Juan.*	5. I don't see.
6. *Creo que no.*	6. I don't know anything.
7. *No tan de prisa.*	7. I've never seen him.
8. *No sé nada.*	8. He doesn't see John.
9. *No veo nada.*	9. I'll never say it.
10. *Nunca le he visto.*	10. He never comes.
11. *No me importa.*	11. I see nothing.
12. *No ha pasado nada.*	12. I'll never go.
13. *Nunca viene.*	13. It's nothing.
14. *No está mal.*	14. He's not here.
15. *Jamás iré.*	15. I don't think so.
16. *No está aquí.*	16. It's not bad.
17. *Nadie viene.*	17. I don't care.
18. *Ni esto ni aquello.*	18. Not so fast.
19. *No se lo diga.*	19. I never go.
20. *No tengo tiempo.*	20. No one comes.

ANSWERS

1—5; 2—13; 3—9; 4—19; 5—8; 6—15; 7—18; 8—6;
9—11; 10—7; 11—17; 12—4; 13—10; 14—16; 15—
12; 16—14; 17—20; 18—1; 19—3; 20—2.

LESSON 24

(Useful Word Groups III)

Dénos unos cuantos.
Give us some.

Déle algunos.
Give him a few.

Algunos amigos míos.
Some of my friends.

3. Like, As, How

Como.
Like, as, how.

Como yo.
Like me.

Como eso.
Like that.

Como esto.
Like this.

Como nosotros.
Like us.

Como los demás.
Like the others.

Éste no es como ése.
This one isn't like that one.

Así es como es.
That's how it is. That's the way it is.

Como usted quiera.
As you wish.

Es como en casa.
It's like (being) home.

No es como su padre.
He's not like his father.

Ignoro cómo explicarlo.
I don't know how to explain it.

¿Cómo es?
What does it look like? ("How is it?")

Es blanco como la nieve.
It's as white as snow.

¡Cómo llueve!
What a rain! ("How it's raining!")

¿Cómo?
What? What did you say? What do you mean?

¿Cómo no?
Why not? Yes, of course.

QUIZ 20

1. *Como usted quiera.*	1. He's not like his father.
2. *Como los demás.*	2. What? What did you say?
3. *Como esto.*	3. Give him a few.
4. *¿Tiene algún dinero?*	4. Why not?
5. *Algunos amigos míos.*	5. Do you want some fruit?
6. *No es como su padre.*	6. As you wish.
7. *¿Cómo?*	7. Does he have any money? Do you have money?
8. *Déle algunos.*	8. Like the others.
9. *¿Cómo no?*	9. Like this.
10. *¿Quiere usted algo de fruta?*	10. Some of my friends.

ANSWERS

1—6; 2—8; 3—9; 4—7; 5—10; 6—1; 7—2; 8—3; 9—4; 10—5.

49. HAVE YOU TWO MET?

¿Conoce usted a mi amigo?
Do you know my friend?

Creo que ya nos hemos conocido.
I believe we've met before.

No creo que haya tenido el gusto.
I don't believe I've had the pleasure.

No tengo el gusto de conocerle.
I haven't had the pleasure ("of meeting you.")

Creo que ustedes ya se conocen, ¿verdad?
I think you already know one another. ("I believe you already know one another, don't you?")

Ya lo creo que nos conocemos.
Of course we know one another.

No tengo el gusto.
I haven't had the pleasure.

Ya he tenido el gusto de conocerle.
I've already had the pleasure of meeting him.

Permítame que le presente a mi amigo Antonio de Alarcón.
Allow me to introduce you to my friend, Antonio de Alarcón.

50. SMALL TALK

Buenos días.
Good morning. Good afternoon. Good day.

Muy buenos días.
("A very") Good morning.

¿Cómo le va?
How are you getting along?

Regular. ¿Y a usted?
So, so. And you?

¿Y a usted cómo le va?
And how are you getting along?

¿Qué novedades hay?
What's new?

Ninguna.
Nothing much.

¿Qué hay de nuevo?
What's new?

Nada de particular.
Nothing much.

LESSON 25

(Small Talk)

¿Hay algo de nuevo?
("Is there") Anything new?

No hay nada de nuevo.
There's nothing new.

¿Qué le pasa que no se le ve?
Where have you been? ("What has happened that no one sees you?")

He estado muy ocupado estos días.
I've been very busy these days.

No deje de telefonearme de vez en cuando.
Give me a ring once in a while.

Le telefonearé un día de estos.
I'll phone you one of these days.

¿Por qué no viene por casa?
Why don't you come to see us ("to our house")?

Iré a visitarles la semana que viene.
I'll call on you next week. ("I'll come to visit you.")

Que no se le olvide lo prometido.
Now don't forget your ("the") promise.

Entonces hasta la semana que viene.
Until next week then.

Hasta la semana que viene.
See you next week. ("Until next week.")

51. TAKING LEAVE

Me alegro mucho de conocerle.
Glad (happy) to have met you.

Encantado.
Glad (happy) to have met you. ("Charmed.")

Espero volver a verle pronto.
Hope to see you again soon.

Así lo espero yo.
I hope so. ("So do I hope it.")

Aquí tiene usted mis señas y mi teléfono.
Here's my address and telephone number.

¿Tiene usted mis señas?
Do you have my address?

No, démelas usted.
No, let me have it.

Notice that the feminine plural form *las* is used because it refers to the feminine plural noun *las señas*.

Aquí las tiene.
Here it is.

Muchas gracias.
Thanks.

¿Cuándo se le puede telefonear a usted?
When can I phone you?

Por las mañanas.
In the morning.

Le llamaré a usted pasado mañana.
I'll call you the day after tomorrow.

Esperaré su llamada.
I'll be expecting your call.

Hasta pronto.
So long.

Hasta más ver.
See you soon.

Hasta la vista.
So long. See you soon.

Hasta luego.
So long. See you later.

Hasta otro rato.
So long. See you again. ("Until another time.")

Hasta mañana.
See you tomorrow. ("Till tomorrow.")

Hasta el sábado.
See you Saturday. ("Till Saturday.")

Adiós.
Good-by.

QUIZ 21

1. *Espero volver a verle pronto.*	1. Do you have my address?
2. *Adiós.*	2. See you tomorrow.
3. *Me alegro mucho de conocerle.*	3. I'll be expecting your call.
4. *¿Tiene usted mis señas?*	4. Till Saturday.
5. *Encantado.*	5. In the morning.
6. *Por las mañanas.*	6. Glad to have met you.
7. *Hasta mañana.*	7. Thanks a lot.
8. *Esperaré su llamada.*	8. Hope to see you soon.
9. *Muchas gracias.*	9. Happy to have met you.
10. *Hasta el sábado.*	10. Good-by.

ANSWERS

1—8; 2—10; 3—6; 4—1; 5—6; 6—5; 7—2; 8—3; 9—7; 10—4.

LESSON 26

52. CALLING ON SOMEONE

(Calling On Someone)

¿Vive aquí el señor Juan García?
Does Mr. John Garcia live here?

Aquí vive.
Yes, he does. ("He lives here.")

¿En qué piso?
On what floor?

Tercero izquierda.
Third floor left.

¿Está en casa el señor García?
Is Mr. Garcia at home?

No, señor. Ha salido.
No, sir. He's gone out.

¿A qué hora volverá?
What time will he be back?

No se lo puedo decir.
I can't tell you.

¿Desea dejarle un recado?
Do you want to leave him a message?

Le dejaré una nota, si me permite un lápiz y un pedazo de papel.
I'll leave him a note, if I may borrow ("if you will permit me") a pencil and a piece of paper from you.

Volveré más tarde.
I'll come back later.

Volveré por la noche.
I'll come back tonight.

Volveré mañana.
I'll come back tomorrow.

Volveré otro día.
I'll come back another day.

Haga el favor de decirle que telefonee.
Please tell him to phone.

Estaré en casa todo el día.
I'll be at home all day.

53. LETTERS AND TELEGRAMS

Quisiera escribir una carta.
I'd like to write a letter.

¿Me puede dar un poco de papel?
Could you let me have ("give me") some paper?

Aquí tiene papel y tinta.
Here's some paper and ink.

Voy al correo.
I'm going to the post office.

¿Dónde venden sellos?
Where are stamps sold?

¿Tiene usted sellos?
Do you have stamps?

Necesito un sello para el correo aéreo.
I need an airmail stamp.

Aquí hay sellos.
Here are some stamps.

Un sello de urgencia, por favor.
A special delivery stamp, please.

¿Donde está el buzón?
Where is the mailbox?

He de poner un telegrama.
I have to send a telegram.

¿Cuánto cuesta un telegrama para Valencia?
How much does a telegram to Valencia cost?

QUIZ 22

1. *Tercero izquierda.*
2. *Volveré más tarde.*
3. *¿Vive aquí el señor Juan Garcia?*
4. *Aquí tiene papel y tinta.*

5. *Quisiera escribir una carta.*
6. *¿Tiene Ud. sellos?*
7. *¿Qué piso?*
8. *Un sello de urgencia.*
9. *Estaré en casa todo el día.*
10. *¿Dónde está el buzón?*

1. I'll be at home all day.
2. Do you have stamps?
3. I'd like to write a letter.
4. Where is the mailbox?
5. What floor?
6. A special delivery stamp.
7. Here's some paper and ink.
8. Does Mr. Juan Garcia live here?
9. Third floor left.
10. I'll come back later.

ANSWERS

1—9; 2—10; 3—8; 4—7; 5—3; 6—2; 7—5; 8—6;
9—1; 10—4.

54. GETTING AROUND

¿Dónde está esta calle?
Where is this street?

¿Cómo se va a este lugar?
How do you get to this place?

¿Está muy lejos?
Is it very far?

¿Cuál es el camino más corto para ir a Madrid?
What's the shortest way to get to Madrid?

¿Qué camino debo tomar?
Which road must I take?

¿Puede usted dirigirme a la calle de Alcalá?
Can you direct me to Alcala Street?

¿Está cerca de aquí la calle Mayor?
Is Main Street near here?

LESSON 27

(Getting Around)

¿Dónde hay un teléfono público?
Where is there a public phone?

¿Dónde puedo telefonear?
Where can I phone?

¿Cuántas cuadras hay de aquí a la estación?
How many blocks away is the station?

¿A qué distancia está la estación?
How far is the station?

¿Estamos todavía lejos de la estación?
Are we still far from the station?

¡Taxi!
Taxi!

¿Está Ud. libre?
Are you taken? (Are you free?)

Lléveme a estas señas.
Take me to this address.

¿Qué le debo?
How much do I owe you?

¿Para aquí el autobús?
Does the bus stop here?

¿Para aquí el tranvía?
Does the streetcar stop here?

¿En qué parada debo apearme?
What stop do I get off?

QUIZ 23

1. ¿Cuál es el camino más corto para ir a . . . ?
2. ¿Dónde puedo telefonear?
3. ¿Dónde está esta calle?
4. Lléveme a estas señas.
5. ¿A qué distancia está la estación?
6. ¿Me permite usar su teléfono?
7. ¿Puede usted dirigirme a la calle . . . ?
8. ¿En qué parada debo apearme?
9. ¿Cómo se va a este lugar?
10. ¿Para aquí el autobús?

1. How far is the station?
2. How do you get to this place?
3. Can you direct me to . . . street?
4. Does the bus stop here?
5. What stop do I get off?
6. Where can I phone?
7. Where is this street?
8. What's the shortest way to get to . . . ?
9. Take me to this address.
10. May I use your telephone?

ANSWERS

1—8; 2—6; 3—7; 4—9; 5—1; 6—10; 7—3; 8—5; 9—2; 10—4.

55. PLEASE

The commonest way of saying "please" is *Haga usted el favor*, which literally means "Do the favor of." Notice how the pronouns are used:

Haga usted el favor de entrar.
Please come in.

Haga el favor de llevar esto.
Please carry this.

Hágame usted el favor de venir.
Please come. ("Do me the favor of coming.")

Háganos usted el favor de entrar.
Please come in. ("Do us the favor of coming in.")

Hagan ustedes el favor de entrar.
Please come in (speaking to several people).

Hágame usted el favor de sus documentos.
Please let me see your papers. ("Do me the
   favor...")

¿Me hace el favor de llamar un taxi?
Will you please call a taxi? ("Will you do me the
   favor...?")

Other polite expressions are:

1. **Tenga la bondad.**
   Please ("have the goodness").
   **Tenga la bondad de decirme dónde queda la
   estación.**
   Please tell me where the station is.

2. **Dispense usted.**
   Excuse me. Pardon me.
   Dispense mi tardanza.
   Excuse my lateness.

3. **Por favor.**
   Please.
   Su boleto, por favor.
   Your ticket, please.
   Siéntese aquí, por favor.
   Please sit here.

4. **Sírvase.**
   Please.
   Sírvase hacerlo lo más pronto posible.
   Please do it as soon as possible.
   ¿Sírvase decirme dónde está la biblioteca?
   Please tell me where the library is.

QUIZ 24

1. *Siéntese aquí, por favor.*
2. *Hágame usted el favor de venir.*
3. *¿Me hace usted el favor de llamar un taxi?*
4. *Dispense mi tardanza.*
5. *Dispense usted.*
6. *Haga usted el favor de entrar.*
7. *Tenga la bondad de decirme dónde queda la estación.*
8. *Haga el favor de llevar esto.*
9. *Su boleto, por favor.*
10. *Sírvase decirme dónde está la biblioteca.*

1. Excuse my lateness.
2. Excuse me. Pardon me.
3. Please come.
4. Please carry this.
5. Please tell me where the library is.

6. Your ticket, please.
7. Will you please call a taxi?
8. Please come in.
9. Can you please tell me where the station is?
10. Please sit here.

ANSWERS

1—10; 2—3; 3—7; 4—1; 5—2; 6—8; 7—9; 8—4;
9—6; 10—5.

56. SOME USEFUL EXPRESSIONS

1. **Acabar de** means "to have just":

Acaba de llegar.
He just came.

Acabo de terminar mi trabajo.
I've just finished my work.

Juan acababa de salir cuando yo llegué.
John had just gone out when I came (arrived).

2. **Tener que** means "to have to":

Tengo que ir.   I have to go.

LESSON 28

(Who, What, When?)

Tengo que irme.   I have to leave.
3. **Hay** means "there is" or "there are":

Hay mucha gente aquí.
There are a lot of people here.

4. **Quisiera** means "I should like to":

¿Quisiera usted sentarse aquí?
Would you like to sit here?

Quisiera ir pero no puedo.
I'd like to go but I can't.

REVIEW QUIZ 5

1. *¿Está en* _____ (home, house) *el señor García?*
   a. *piso*
   b. *hora*
   c. *casa*

2. *¿Desea dejarle un* _____ (message)?
   a. *lápiz*
   b. *recado*
   c. *papel*

3. *¿Dónde está esta* _____ (street)?
   a. *lugar*
   b. *camino*
   c. *calle*

4. _____ (I need) *un sello para el correo aéreo.*
   a. *venden*
   b. *necesito*
   c. *urgencia*

5. *¿* _____ (who) *ha dicho eso?*
   a. *que*
   b. *quién*
   c. *cuyo*

6. _____ (because) *no quiero perder el tren.*
   a. *porque*
   b. *para que*
   c. *que*

7. *¿De* _____ (what) *hablaban ustedes?*
   a. *por qué*
   b. *qué*
   c. *desea*

8. *¿*_____ (which) *quiere usted?*
   a. *qué*
   b. *por que*
   c. *cuál*

9. *Tenga la* _____ *de decirme dónde queda la estación.*
   a. *dispense*
   b. *bondad*
   c. *haga*

10. *Hagan ustedes el* _____ *de entrar.*
    a. *bondad*
    b. *favor*
    c. *sírvase*

11. _____ (please) *hacerlo lo más pronto posible.*
    a. *sírvase*
    b. *dispense*
    c. *favor*

12. _____ (I've just) *de terminar mi trabajo.*
    a. *llegar*
    b. *acabo*
    c. *acaba*

13. _____ (I should like) *ir pero no puedo.*
    a. quisiera
    b. acaba
    c. quiero

14. ¿_____ (why) *no se lo dice usted?*
    a. qué
    b. por qué
    c. quién

ANSWERS
1 c.; 2 b.; 3 c.; 4 c.; 5 b.; 6 a.; 7 b.; 8 c.; 9 b.; 10 b.;
11 a.; 12 b.; 13 a.; 14 b.; 15 a.

57. WHO? WHAT? WHEN?

1. *¿Quién?* "Who?"

¿Quién es?	Who is he (she)?
No sé quien es.	I dont know who he is.
¿Quiénes son?	Who are they?
¿Quién lo ha dicho?	Who said it?
¿Quién ha dicho eso?	Who said so?
¿Quién lo ha hecho?	Who did it?
¿De quién es este lápiz?	Whose pencil is this?
¿Para quién es esto?	Who is this for?
¿A quién quiere ver usted?	Who(m) do you wish to see?
¿A quién quiere hablar?	To whom do you wish to speak?
¿Quién sabe?	Who knows?
¿A quién pertenece esto?	Whose is this?

2. *¿Qué?* "What?"

¿Qué es esto?	What's this?
¿Qué es eso?	What's that?

¿Qué pasa?	What's the matter? What's up?
¿Qué sucede?	What's the matter? What's up?
¿Qué sucedió?	What happened?
¿Qué hay de nuevo?	What's new?
¿Qué le parece?	What do you think?
¿Qué son?	What are they?
¿Qué tienen ustedes?	What do you have? What's the matter with you?
¿Qué hora es?	What time is it?
¿Qué dice usted?	What are you saying?
¿Qué ha dicho usted?	What did you say?
¿De qué hablan ustedes?	What are you talking about?
¿De qué se trata?	What's it all about? What's the point?
¿Qué quiere?	What do you want?
¿Qué desea usted?	What can I do for you? What do you wish?

3. *¿Por qué?* "Why?"

¿Por qué así	Why so?
¿Por qué no?	Why not?
¿Por qué razón?	For what reason?
¿Por qué lo dice usted?	Why do you say that?
¿Por qué tanta prisa?	Why are you in such a hurry? Why the hurry?
¿Por qué lo ha hecho usted?	Why did you do it?

4. *¿Cómo?* "How?"

| ¿Cómo se dice en español esto? | How do you say this in Spanish? |

¿Cómo se llama usted?	What is your name? ("How do you call yourself?")
¿Cómo se escribe eso?	How is this written (spelled)?

5. *¿Cuánto?* "How Much?"

¿Cuánto dinero necesita usted?	How much money do you need?
¿Cuántos libros hay?	How many books are there?
¿Cuánto hay de Madrid a Barcelona?	How far is it from Madrid to Barcelona?

LESSON 29

(Liking and Disliking)

6. *¿Cuál?* "What?" "Which?"

¿Cuál es su nombre?	What is his name?
¿Cuál quiere usted?	Which (one) do you want?
¿Cuál quiere, éste o aquél?	Which (one) do you want, this or that one?
¿Cuál de estos lápices es de usted?	Which one of these pencils is yours?
¿Cuál de los dos caminos conduce a Madrid?	Which of these two roads leads to Madrid?
¿Cuáles son sus señas?	What's his address? *Or* What's your address?

7. *¿Dónde?* "Where?"

¿Dónde está su amigo?	Where is your friend?
¿Dónde vive,él?	Where does he live?
¿Dónde va ella?	Where is she going?

8. *¿Cuándo?* "When?"

¿Cuándo vendrá su hermano?	When will your brother come?
¿Cuándo ocurrió eso?	When did that happen?
¿Cuándo se marcha usted?	When are you going (leaving)?
No sé cuando.	I don't know when.
¿Hasta cuándo?	Until when? How long?
No sé hasta cuando.	I don't know until when. I don't know how long.
¿Para cuándo?	How soon?
Para cuando usted quiera.	As soon as you like.
¿Desde cuándo?	Since when?
¿Desde cuándo acá?	Since when? How come? How's that?

QUIZ 25

1. *¿Cómo se llama usted?*	1. When did that happen?
2. *¿Cuántos libros hay?*	2. Since when?
3. *¿Cómo se dice esto en español?*	3. Who knows?
4. *¿Qué dice usted?*	4. Where does he live?
5. *¿Cuándo ocurrió eso?*	5. What's your name?
6. *¿Desde cuándo?*	6. What are you saying?
7. *¿Quién sabe?*	7. Why not?
8. *¿Por qué no?*	8. How do you write that?
9. *¿Dónde vive él?*	9. How many books are there?
10. *¿Cómo se escribe eso?*	10. How do you say this in Spanish?

ANSWERS

1—5; 2—9; 3—10; 4—6; 5—1; 6—2; 7—3; 8—7;
9—4; 10—8.

REVIEW QUIZ 6

1. No veo _____ (nothing).
    a. nadie
    b. nada
    c. nunca

2. No viene _____ (nobody).
    a. nadie
    b. no
    c. nunca

3. No sabe leer _____ (nor) *escribir.*
    a. no
    b. jamás
    c. ni

4. El español es fácil _____ (isn't it?).
    a. verdad
    b. no es verdad
    c. no

5. Déme usted unos _____ (a few).
    a. nada
    b. cuantos
    c. algo

6. Quiere usted _____ (some) *de fruta?*
    a. algunos
    b. cuantos
    c. algo

7. *No es* _____ (like) *su padre.*
   a. *como*
   b. *esto*
   c. *demás*

8. *He estado muy* _____ (busy) *estos días.*
   a. *siempre*
   b. *ocupado*
   c. *nuevo*

9. *¿Se* _____ (know) *ustedes?*
   a. *conocido*
   b. *conocen*
   c. *conocerle*

10. *¿A quien tengo el gusto de* _____ (speak)?
    a. *hablar*
    b. *tengo*
    c. *conocer*

11. *Aquí tiene usted mis* _____ (address) *y mi teléfono.*
    a. *día*
    b. *tarjeta*
    c. *señas*

12. *A ver si nos vemos un* _____ (day) *de estos.*
    a. *día*
    b. *muy*
    c. *semana*

13. *Aquí tiene usted la* _____ (mine).
    a. *muy*
    b. *mía*
    c. *día*

14. ¿_____ (what) *dice usted?*
    a. *cómo*
    b. *cuándo*
    c. *qué*

15. ¿_____ (why) *se fué ella?*
    a. *qué*
    b. *por qué*
    c. *cuánto*

16. ¿_____ (how) *se dice en español esto?*
    a. *cómo*
    b. *cuándo*
    c. *nadie*

17. ¿_____ (how much) *dinero necesita usted?*
    u. *quién*
    b. *cuánto*
    c. *cuyo*

18. ¿_____ (who) *vino con usted?*
    a. *quién*
    b. *cuyo*
    c. *cuál*

19. ¿_____ (where) *está su amigo?*
    a. *dónde*
    b. *cómo*
    c. *qué*

20. ¿_____ (when) *vendrá su hermano?*
    a. *quién*
    b. *cuál*
    c. *cuando*

58. LIKING AND DISLIKING

1. I Like It

Bueno.	Good.
Muy bueno.	Very good.
Es muy bueno.	It's very good.
Es excelente.	It's excellent.
Es estupendo.	It's wonderful.
Es magnífico.	It's excellent. It's wonderful.
Es admirable.	It's excellent. It's admirable.
Es perfecto.	It's perfect.
Está bien.	It's all right.
No está mal.	It's not bad.
¿Está bien esto?	Is it all right?
¡Muy bien!	Very well! Very good!
Es bella.	She's beautiful.
Es bellísima.	She's very beautiful.
Es muy linda.	She's very pretty.
Es encantadora.	She's charming.
¡Qué bonito!	How pretty!
¡Qué lindo!	How pretty!
¡Qué bueno!	How nice!
¡Qué hermoso!	How beautiful!

2. I Don't Like It

No es bueno.	It's not good. It's no good.

No es muy bueno.	It's not very good.
Eso no es bueno.	That's no good.
Esto no está bien.	It's not right. This isn't right. This isn't proper. This is wrong.
Eso es malo.	That's bad.
Es bastante malo.	It's (he's) very bad.
Eso es pésimo.	That's bad. That's awfully bad.
Eso es malísimo.	That's very bad.
Es verdaderamente malo.	He's (it's) really ("truly") bad.
No me interesa.	I don't care for it. It doesn't interest me.
No me gusta.	I don't like it.

LESSON 30

(I Like)

No me gusta nada.	I don't like it at all.
Eso no vale nada.	That's worthless.
No sirve para nada.	It's worthless. It's good for nothing.
¡Qué lastima!	What a pity!
¡Qué desgracia!	How unfortunate! ("What a misfortune!")
¡Qué horror!	How awful!

QUIZ 26

1. *Está bien.*	1. It's excellent.
2. *Muy bien.*	2. She's very pretty.
3. *Es excelente.*	3. That's worthless!
4. *No está mal.*	4. What a pity!
5. *Eso es malo.*	5. How unfortunate!
6. *¡Qué lástima!*	6. It's wonderful!
7. *Es muy linda.*	7. It's all right.
8. *Eso no vale nada.*	8. That's bad.
9. *¡Qué desgracia!*	9. Very well.
10. *Es estupendo.*	10. It's not bad.

ANSWERS

1—7; 2—9; 3—1; 4—10; 5—8; 6—4; 7—2; 8—3; 9—5; 10—6.

3. I Like

Me gusta . . .	I like . . . ("It pleases me . . .")
Me gusta.	I like it (him, her).
Me gusta mucho.	I like it (him, her) very much.
Me gusta muchísimo.	I like it (him, her) very much.
Eso me gusta.	I like that.
Ella me gusta.	I like her.
Me gustan mucho.	I like them a lot.
¿Le gusta?	Do you like it?
¿No le gusta?	Don't you like it?
¿Le gusta a usted la fruta?	Do you like fruit?
Sí, me gusta la fruta.	Yes, I like fruit.
¿Les gusta el chocolate?	Do you *(pl.)* like chocolate?
¿Le gusta América?	Do you like America?
¿Le gustan los Estados Unidos?	Do you like the United States?

¿Le gusta la comida española?	Do you like Spanish food?
¿Le gusta España?	Do you like Spain?
¿Le ha gustado España?	Did you like Spain?
¿Me gustó España.	I liked Spain.
¿Cree que les gustará la casa?	Do you think they'll like the house?
¿Cómo les gusta mi cuarto?	How do you like my room? *(speaking to several people)*
Me gusta.	I like it.
Me gusta mucho.	I like it very much.
No me gusta.	I don't like it.
No me gusta mucho.	I don't like it very much.
Si a usted le gusta.	If you like it.
Cuando usted guste.	Whenever you like.
Yo gusto de la música.[1]	I'm fond of music.

Notice that the Spanish for "I like fruit" is *Me gusta la fruta* ("To me is pleasing fruit"). That is, the word which is the object in English is the subject in Spanish. "I like the United States" is *Me gustan los Estados Unidos* ("To me are pleasing the United States"). Here the verb is plural because the subject is plural.

[1]The tape should properly state: *Me gusta la música.*

QUIZ 27

1. ¿Le gusta la comida española?	1. I don't like it very much.
2. ¿Le gusta?	2. How do you like my room?
3. Me gusta mucho.	3. Did you like Spain?
4. ¿Le gusta a usted la fruta?	4. If you like it.
5. Cuando usted guste.	5. Don't you like it?
6. ¿Le gustó España?	6. I like it very much.
7. ¿No le gusta?	7. Do you like it?
8. Si a usted le gusta.	8. Whenever you like.
9. No me gusta mucho.	9. Do you like Spanish food?
10. ¿Cómo les gusta mi cuarto?	10. Do you like fruit?

ANSWERS

1—9; 2—7; 3—6; 4—10; 5—8; 6—3; 7—5; 8—4; 9—1; 10—2.

59. IN, TO, FROM

He estado en Madrid.	I've been in Madrid.
Voy a Madrid.	I'm going to Madrid.
Vengo de Madrid.	I come (am) from Madrid.
Salgo para Madrid.	I'm leaving for Madrid.
Se dirige hacia Madrid.	He's going towards Madrid.
Llegué hasta Madrid.	I got as far as Madrid.

1. *A* "to," "by," "at," "on," "in"

A la derecha.	To the right.
A la izquierda.	To the left.

Dos a dos.	Two by two.
Poco a poco.	Little by little.
A pie.	On foot.
A mano.	By hand.
A mediodía.	At noon.
A medianoche.	At midnight.
Se sentaron a la mesa.	They sat down to the table.
A la española.	In the Spanish manner.

When the direct object refers to a definite person or is the name of a person or place, *a* is used before it:

Acabo de ver a mi amigo.	I have just seen my friend.
Veo a Juan.	I see John.
Visito a Madrid.	I'm visiting Madrid.

LESSON 31

(Useful Word Groups IV)

2. *Con* "with"

Café con leche.	Coffee with milk.
Yo fuí con Juan.	I went with John.
Lo escribió con un lápiz.	He wrote it with a pencil.

3. *De* "of," "from"

Es de mi hermano.	It's from my brother.
Vengo de Madrid.	I come (am) from Madrid.
Es de madera.	It's made of wood.
De día.	By day. In the daytime.
De nuevo.	Again.

4. *En* "in"

Viví en México por varios años.	I lived in Mexico for several years.
Me voy en cuatro días.	I'm leaving in four days.
En lugar de.	In place of.
En vez de.	Instead.

5. *Hasta* "up to," "until"

Hasta Buenos Aires.	Up to (as far as) Buenos Aires.
Caminé hasta el quinto piso.	I walked up to the fifth floor.
Hasta mañana.	Until tomorrow.
Hasta luego.	See you soon. ("Until soon.")
Hasta más tarde.	See you later. ("Until later.")
Hasta la vista.	Au revoir. Until we see each other again.

6. *Hacia* "towards"

Hacia allí.	In that direction.
Ella caminaba hacia el parque.	She was walking toward (in the direction of) the park.
Empezó a llover hacia la noche.	It started to rain towards night.

7. *Desde* "from"

Desde Barcelona hasta Madrid.	From Barcelona to Madrid.
Desde que le ví.	Since I saw him. Since the time I saw him.

8. *Sobre* "on"

Sobre la mesa.	On the table.
Tenía un pañuelo sobre la cabeza.	She had a handkerchief on her head.

9. *Por* "for" "through"

Sesenta millas por hora.	Sixty miles an hour.
Lo compré por un dólar.	I bought it for a dollar.
Le dí un peso por esto.	I gave him a dollar for this.
Me dió su libro por el mío.	He exchanged books with me. He gave me his book for mine.
Pasamos por México.	We passed through Mexico.
El tren pasa por Madrid.	The train passes through Madrid.
Entró por la puerta.	He came in through the door.
Yo iré por usted.	I'll go for (in place of) you.
Fué por el médico.	He went for the doctor.
Estaré de viaje por dos años.	I'll be away traveling for two years.

Other Expressions:

¿Por qué?	Why? What was the reason?
Por ahora.	For the time being.
Por la mañana.	In the morning. During the morning.
Mañana por la mañana.	Tomorrow morning.
Mañana por la tarde.	Tomorrow afternoon.
Por la tarde.	During the afternoon. In the afternoon.
Por la noche.	At night.
Pasó por la calle.	He walked along the street.
Por ejemplo.	For example.
Por consiguiente.	Consequently. As a result.

Por lo general.	In general.
Por completo.	Completely.
Por eso.	For that reason.
Por razón de.	By reason of.
Por causa de.	On account of.
Por fín.	Finally. At last.
Por aquí.	Around here.
No estoy por ir.	I'm not in favor of doing it.
Estoy por hacerlo.	I'm in favor of doing it.
¡Por Dios!	For goodness' sake! For heaven's sake!

10. *Para* "for" "in order to"

Para indicates direction, purpose:

Para ir allá.	In order to go there.
Un estante para libros.	A bookcase ("a stand for books").
Salió para la Habana.	He left for Havana.
El autobús para Madrid.	The bus for Madrid.
La carta es para usted.	The letter is for you.
La lección para mañana.	The lesson for tomorrow.
Para él, eso es fácil.	That's easy for him.
No sirve para nada.	It's worthless. It's good for nothing.
Estudio para médico.	I'm studying to be a doctor.

With *estar* it means "about to":

Está para llover.	It's about to rain.
Estábamos para salir.	We were about to leave.
Está para ir.	He's about to go. He's ready to go.

QUIZ 28

1. *A mediodía.*	1. On foot.
2. *Poco a poco.*	2. One by one.
3. *A la derecha.*	3. I come from Madrid.
4. *A la española.*	4. It's made of wood.
5. *Con.*	5. By day.
6. *A pie.*	6. Again.
7. *Vengo de Madrid.*	7. On the table.
8. *Es de madera.*	8. To the right.
9. *En cuanto a.*	9. In that direction.
10. *De nuevo.*	10. Little by little.
11. *Hacia allí.*	11. Until tomorrow.
12. *De día.*	12. At noon.
13. *A la izquierda.*	13. Since I saw him.
14. *Uno a uno.*	14. In the Spanish manner.
15. *Hasta Buenos Aires.*	15. With.
16. *Me voy en dos días.*	16. Instead of.
17. *Sobre la mesa.*	17. To the left.
18. *Hasta mañana.*	18. In regard to.
19. *En vez de.*	19. As far as Buenos Aires.
20. *Desde que le ví.*	20. I'm leaving in two days.

ANSWERS

1—12; 2—10; 3—8; 4—14; 5—15; 6—1; 7—3; 8—4;
9—18; 10—6; 11—9; 12—5; 13—17; 14—2; 15—19;
16—20; 17—7; 18—11; 19—16; 20—13.

QUIZ 29

1. Por ejemplo.	1. I gave him a dollar for this.
2. El tren pasa por Madrid.	2. Sixty miles an hour.
3. Pasamos por México.	3. Completely.
4. Por ahora.	4. For that reason.
5. Lo compré por un dólar.	5. Around here.
6. Por eso.	6. For goodness' sake!
7. Sesenta millas por hora.	7. At last.
8. Por completo.	8. For example.
9. Le dí un peso por esto.	9. I'm not in favor of going.
10. ¡Por Dios!	10. For the time being.
11. Por fin.	11. I bought it for a dollar.
12. Entró por la puerta.	12. The train passes through Madrid.
13. Por aquí.	13. I'll go for you.
14. Yo iré por usted.	14. He came in through the door.
15. No estoy por ir.	15. We passed through Mexico.

ANSWERS

1—8; 2—12; 3—15; 4—10; 5—11; 6—4; 7—2; 8—3; 9—1; 10—6; 11—7; 12—14; 13—5; 14—13; 15—9.

QUIZ 30

1. La carta es para usted.	1. A bookcase.
2. No sirve para nada.	2. The lesson for tomorrow.

3. *La lección para mañana.*	3. In order to go there.
4. *Está para llover.*	4. He left for Havana.
5. *Estoy por hacerlo.*	5. I'm studying to be a doctor.
6. *Un estante para libros.*	6. He's about to leave.
7. *Para ir allá.*	7. The letter is for you.
8. *Salió para la Habana.*	8. I'm in favor of doing it.
9. *Está para ir.*	9. It's worthless.
10. *Estudio para médico.*	10. It's about to rain.

ANSWERS

1—7; 2—9; 3—2; 4—10; 5—8; 6—1; 7—3; 8—4; 9—6; 10—5.

LESSON 32

60. ASKING YOUR WAY

(Asking Your Way)

Perdón.
Pardon me. Excuse me.
Perdóneme.
Pardon me.
Dispénseme.
Excuse me.
¿Cómo se llama este pueblo?
What is the name of this town?
¿A qué distancia estamos de Madrid?
How far are we from Madrid?
¿Cuántos kilómetros hay de aquí a Madrid?
How many kilometers from here to Madrid?

Está a diez kilómetros de aquí.
It's ten kilometers from here.

Está a veinte kilómetros de aquí.
It's twenty kilometers from here.

¿Cómo puedo ir desde aquí a Madrid?
How do I get to Madrid from here?

Siga este camino.
Follow this road.

¿Puede usted decirme cómo ir a estas señas?
Can you tell me how I can get to this address?

¿Puede usted decirme cómo ir a este lugar?
Can you tell me how I can get to this place?

¿Cómo se llama esta calle?
What is the name of this street?

¿Puede usted decirme dónde queda esta calle?
Can you tell me where this street is?

¿Dónde está la calle de Hortaleza?
Where is Hortaleza Street?

¿Está lejos de aquí?
Is it far from here?

¿Está cerca de aquí?
Is it near here?

Es la tercera bocacalle a la derecha.
It's the third block to the right.

Vaya por aquí.
Go this way.

Siga todo derecho.
Go straight ahead.

Siga hasta la esquina y doble a la izquierda.
Go to the corner and turn left.

Tome la primera bocacalle a la izquierda.
Take the first street to the left.

Doble a la derecha.
Turn right.

¿Dónde está el garage?
Where is the garage?

¿Dónde está la comisaría?
Where is the police station?

¿Dónde está el ayuntamiento?
Where is City Hall?

¿Dónde está la parada del autobús?
Where is the bus stop?

¿En qué parada debo apearme?
What station do I get off?

¿Dónde debo apearme?
Where do I get off?

¿Dónde está la estación del ferrocarril?
Where is the railroad station?

¿Cuál es la estación para ir a Madrid?
Where do you get the train for Madrid? (''Which is
the station to go to Madrid?'')

¿De qué estación sale el tren para Madrid?
From which station does the train to Madrid leave?

¿A qué estación llega el tren de Madrid?
At which station does the Madrid train arrive?

¿Dónde está el despacho de información?
Where is Information?

¿Quiere darme un horario de trenes?
Will you please let me have a timetable?

¿Cuál es el tren para Madrid?
Which is the train for Madrid?

¿Es éste el tren de Madrid?
Is this the train for Madrid?

¿Dónde se toma el tren para Madrid?
Where do you get the train for Madrid?

En el andén número dos.
On track two.

¿A qué hora sale el tren para Madrid?
When does the train for Madrid leave?

El tren acaba de salir.
The train just left.

El tren va a salir en seguida.
The train is leaving right away.

¿A qué hora sale el próximo tren?
When does the next train leave?

¿Dónde está el despacho de billetes?
Where is the ticket window?

Déme un billete de ida para Madrid.
Give me a one-way ticket to Madrid.

¿De primera o de segunda?
First or second class?

De primera.
First class.

¿Cuánto cuesta?
How much does it cost?

Veinte pesetas y veinticinco céntimos.
Twenty pesetas and twenty-five centimos.

¿Cuánto se tarda en llegar allí?
How long does it take to get there?

LESSON 33

(Asking Your Way)

Un poco más de una hora.
A little more than an hour.

¿Está ocupado este asiento?
Is this seat taken?

¿Me permite usted que ponga aquí esta maleta?
May I put this suitcase here?

¿Qué estación es esta?
What station is this?

Cuánto tiempo paramos aquí?
How long do we stop here?

¿Tengo que cambiar aquí de tren?
Do I change trains here?

¿Para este tren en Madrid?
Does this train stop in Madrid?

61. WRITING, PHONING, TELEGRAPHING

¿Tiene usted un lápiz?
Do you have a pencil?

¿Tiene usted una pluma?
Do you have a pen?

¿Tiene usted un secante?
Do you have a blotter?

¿Tiene usted un sobre?
Do you have an envelope?

¿Tiene usted un sello?
Do you have a stamp?

¿Dónde puedo comprar un sello de correos?
Where can I buy a stamp?

¿Tiene usted un sello para el correo aéreo?
Do you have an airmail stamp?

¿Dónde está el correo?
Where is the post office?

Quiero enviar esta carta.
I'd like to mail this letter.

¿Cuánto es el franqueo?
How many stamps do I need on this letter?

¿Dónde está el buzón más cerca?
Where is the nearest mailbox?

En la esquina.
On the corner.

Quiero poner un telegrama.
I'd like to send a telegram.

¿Dónde está la oficina de telégrafos?
Where is the telegraph office?

Está en correos.
It's in the post office.

¿Cuánto cuesta un telegrama a Madrid?
How much is a telegram to Madrid?

¿Cuánto tarda en llegar allí?
How long does it take to get there?

¿Hay un teléfono aquí?
Is there a phone here?

¿Dónde puedo telefonear?
Where can I phone?

¿Dónde está el teléfono?
Where is the telephone?

¿Dónde está la cabina telefónica?
Where is the phone booth?

En el vestíbulo del hotel.
In the hotel lobby.

¿Me permite usar el teléfono?
May I use your phone?

Desde luego, ¡con mucho gusto!
Of course, go ahead!

Conécteme con el servicio interurbano.
Give me long distance.

¿Cuánto cuesta una llamada telefónica a Madrid?
How much is a phone call to Madrid?

Quiero hablar con el siete-cinco-ocho-dos.
I want 7582.

Espere un momento.
Hold the wire a minute.

La línea está ocupada.
The line is busy.

Señorita, usted me dió el número equivocado.
Operator, you gave me the wrong number.

No contesta nadie.
There is no answer.

¿Puedo hablar con el señor Castro?
May I speak to Mr. Castro?

Al habla. or **Servidor.**
Speaking.

Habla el señor Villanueva.
This is Mr. Villanueva speaking.

¿El señor Castro?
Is this Mr. Castro?

El mismo.
Speaking. ("The same.")

¿Con quién hablo?
Who is this? ("With whom am I speaking?")

Con el señor Castro.
Mr. Castro. ("With Mr. Castro.")

LESSON 34

62. FAMILY AFFAIRS

(Family Affairs)

¿Cómo se llama usted?
What's your name?

Me llamo Juan Castro.
My name is Juan Castro.

¿Cómo se llama él?
What's his name?

El se llama Carlos Pérez.
His name is Carlos Perez.

¿Cómo se llama ella?
What's her name?

Se llama María Fernández.
Her name is Maria Fernandez.

¿Cómo se llaman ellos?
What are their names?

El se llama José Rivera y ella Anita Ferrero.
His name is Jose Rivera and hers is Anita Ferrero.

¿Cuál es su nombre?
What's his first name?

Su nombre es Carlos.
His first name is Carlos.

¿Cuál es su apellido?
What's his last name?

Su apellido es Pérez.
His last name is Perez.

¿De dónde es usted?
Where are you from?

Yo soy de Madrid.
I'm from Madrid.

¿Dónde nació usted?
Where were you born?

Yo nací en Madrid.
I was born in Madrid.

¿Cuántos años tiene usted?
How old are you?

Tengo veinticuatro años.
I'm twenty-four.

Cumplo veinticuatro años en septiembre.
I'll be twenty-four in September.

Nací el diecinueve de agosto de mil novecientos dieciséis.
I was born August 19, 1916.

¿Cuántos hermanos tiene usted?
How many brothers do you have?

Tengo dos hermanos.
I have two brothers.

El mayor tiene veintidós años.
The older one is twenty-two.

Estudia en la Universidad.
He's at the University.

El menor tiene diecisiete años.
The younger one is seventeen.

Está en el último año del Instituto.
He's in his last year of high school.

¿Cuántas hermanas tiene usted?
How many sisters do you have?

Tengo una hermana.
I have one sister.

Tiene nueve años.
She's nine.

Ella va a una escuela primaria.
She goes to grammar (primary) school.

¿Qué es su padre?
What does your father do?

Es abogado.
He's a lawyer.

Es arquitecto.
He's an architect.

Es maestro.
He's a teacher.

Es profesor de la Universidad.
He's a university professor.

Es médico.
He's a doctor.

Es comerciante.
He's a businessman.

Es agricultor.
He's a farmer.

Es funcionario público.
He's in the government service.

Es obrero.
He's a worker.

Trabaja en una fábrica de automóviles.
He works in an automobile factory.

¿Cuándo es su cumpleaños?
When is your birthday?

**Mi cumpleaños es dentro de dos semanas, el
   veintitrés de enero.**
My birthday is in two weeks, January 23.

¿Tiene usted parientes aquí?
Do you have any relatives here?

¿Vive aquí toda su familia?
Does all your family live here?

Toda mi familia menos mis abuelos.
All my family except my grandparents.

Ellos viven en una finca cerca de Toledo.
They live on a farm near Toledo.

¿Es usted pariente del señor Villanueva?
Are you related to Mr. Villanueva?

Es mi tío.
He's my uncle.

Es mi primo.
He's my cousin.

¿Es usted pariente de la señora de García?
Are you related to Mrs. Garcia?

Es mi tía.
She's my aunt.

Es mi prima.
She's my cousin.

LESSON 35

63. DE COMPRAS
BUYING THINGS

(Buying Things. Ordering Breakfast)

1. **¿Qué vale esto?**
   How much is this?

2. **Diez pesetas.**
   Ten pesetas.

3. **Es bastante caro. ¿No tiene usted algo más barato?**
   That's rather expensive. Haven't you anything cheaper?

4. **¿En el mismo género?**
   Of the same sort?

5. **En el mismo género u otro parecido.**
   The same sort or something similar.

6. **Aquí tiene éste.**
   There's this.

7. **¿No tiene usted algo en otra clase que me pueda mostrar?**
   Haven't you any other kind you could show me?

8. **¿De menos precio?**
Less expensive?

9. **Si es posible . . .**
If ("it's") possible.

10. **Acaso sea ésta el que usted quiere.**
Perhaps you would like this?

11. **Depende del precio.**
That depends on the price.

12. **Este vale ocho pesetas.**
This one is eight pesetas.

13. **Me gusta más que el otro.**
I like it better than the other one.

14. **Es más barato.**
It's cheaper.

15. **Y este otro, ¿es más barato o más caro?**
How about this? Is it cheaper or more expensive?

16. **Es más caro.**
It's more expensive.

17. **¿Y no tiene usted más surtido?**
Haven't you anything else in stock?

18. **Estoy esperando recibir algunas novedades en breve.**
I'm hoping to receive some new styles soon.

19. **¿Para cuándo?**
How soon?

20. **De un día a otro. ¿Puede usted pasar por aquí a fines de semana?**
Any day now. Can you drop in towards the end of the week?

21. **Lo haré . . . ¿Y esto que precio tiene?**
I'll do that. . . . What's the price of this?

22. **Cinco pesetas, par.**
Five pesetas a pair.

23. **Déme usted una docena.**
Let me have a dozen.

24. **¿Se los lleva usted misma?**
Will you take them with you? ("Will you take them yourself?")

25. **Prefiero que me los envíe.**
I'd rather have you send them.

26. **¿A las mismas señas de siempre?**
Is the address still the same?

27. **Las mismas.**
The same.

28. **Buenos días.**
Good-by. ("Until another day.")

29. **Adiós.**
Good-by.

NOTES

Title: *De compras* "About (concerning) purchases."[1]

1. [2]*Valer* to be worth, to amount to. *¿Qué vale esto?* ("What is this worth?") How much is this? You can also say: *¿Cuánto vale?* (*¿Cuánto cuesta?*) How much is it? *¿Qué precio tiene?* (*¿Cuál es el precio?*) What's the price? *¿A cómo es eso?* What's the price of that? *¿A cuánto están las naranjas?* (*¿A cómo están las naranjas?*) *¿A cómo vende usted las naranjas?* ("For how much do you sell the oranges?") How much are the oranges?

2. *Es bastante caro* That's rather expensive. *Muy caro* or *carísimo* very expensive (see p. 237).—*Barato* cheap. *Más barato* cheaper (see

[1]Words in quotation marks are literal translations.
[2]Numbers refer to the sentences above.

p. 237). *Muy barato* or *baratísimo* very cheap.

5. *Género* kind, class, sort.

6. "Here you have this."

7. "Haven't you anything in another kind you could show me?" *Muéstreme alguna otra cosa.* Show me something else. You can also say: *Enséñeme alguna otra cosa. Mostrar* and *enseñar* both mean "to show."

8. *De menos precio* "of less price."

10. *Sea* from *ser* (see p. 286).—"Perhaps this is what you want (would like)?"

11. *Depender de* to depend upon.

13. *Me gusta más* I like it more (see p. 128).

15. *Y este otro.* "And this other one."

17. *Surtido* assortment, supply, stock. "And haven't you more stock?"

18. *Estoy esperando* I'm expecting (see p. 283). *Novedad* latest style, latest fashion. *Novedades* new styles. *La última novedad* the latest news; the latest styles. *¿Hay alguna novedad?* Is there anything new? *Sin novedad* as usual; nothing new. *No hay novedad.* There's nothing new.—*En breve* in brief; in a short time.

19. *¿Para cuándo?* "For when?"

20. *De un día a otro* "From one day to the next." *Pasar por aquí* to pass by here, to stop in here.

21. *Lo haré* I'll do that. *Haré* is from *hacer* to make, do (see p. 187).

23. *Déme.* Give me. *Dé* is from *dar* (see p. 190); *me* me. Notice that the *me* is written together with the *dé* (see p. 257).

25. *Prefiero que* . . . I'd prefer that . . . , I'd rather.

26. "The same address as always?" *Las mismas* the same. The form is feminine plural because it refers to *señas* (address) which is feminine plural.

28. *Hasta otro día* "Until another day." Other expressions: *Hasta mañana* "Until tomorrow." *Hasta la vista.* "Until we see one another again." *Hasta luego.* See you soon. *Hasta más ver.* See you later. *Adiós.* Good-by. *Que lo pase usted bien. (Páselo usted bien.)* ("May you get along well.") Good-by. *Quede usted con Dios (Queden ustedes con Dios).* "Remain with God" (said by person leaving). *Vaya usted con Dios (Vayan ustedes con Dios)* "Go with God" (said by person remaining behind).

QUIZ 31

1. *Es bastante* _____ (expensive).
   a. *vale*
   b. *esto*
   c. *caro*

2. *No tiene usted algo más* _____ (cheap).
   a. *género*
   b. *precio*
   c. *barato*

3. *En el* _____ (same) *género.*
   a. *algo*
   b. *mismo*
   c. *más*

4. *De* _____ (less) *precio.*
   a. *más*
   b. *menos*
   c. *mismo*

5. *Me gusta* _____ (more) *que el otro.*
   a. *acaso*
   b. *más*
   c. *vale*

6. ¿No _____ (have) *usted más surtido?*
   a. *tiene*
   b. *caro*
   c. *otro*

7. *Estoy esperando* _____ (receive) *novedades.*
   a. *preferencia*
   b. *tranquilo*
   c. *recibir*

8. ¿*Para* _____ (when)?
   a. *surtido*
   b. *caro*
   c. *cuándo*

9. *A las mismas* _____ (address) *de siempre?*
   a. *señas*
   b. *domicilio*
   c. *envíe*

ANSWERS

1 c; 2 c; 3 b; 4 b; 5 b; 6 a; 7 c; 8 c; 9 a.

64. DESAYUNO
BREAKFAST

1. **P¹: ¿Tendrás apetito?**
   P¹: You must be hungry. ("Do you have an appetite?")

2. **J: Sí que lo tengo.**
   J: I certainly am. ("I certainly have.")

3. **L: Yo tengo una hambre canina.**
   L: I'm terribly hungry.

¹P. stands here for *Pedro* "Peter"; *J.* for *Juan* "John"; *L.* for *Luisa* "Louise"; *M.* for *Mozo* "Waiter."

4. **P: ¡Camarero! ¡Camarero!**
   P: Waiter! Waiter!

5. **M: Díganme los señores.**
   M: Yes, gentlemen.

6. **P: Queremos desayuno para tres personas.**
   P: We'd like breakfast for three.

7. **L: ¿Qué podría servirnos?**
   L: What can you serve us?

8. **M: Café con leche, té con limón o con leche, chocolate ...**
   M: Coffee with milk, tea with lemon or with milk, chocolate ...

9. **P: ¿Con qué lo sirven?**
   P: What do you serve with it?

10. **M: Con panecillos, tostados, bizcochos ...**
    M: Rolls, toast, biscuits ...

11. **L: ¿Hay mantequilla?**
    L: Is there any butter?

12. **M: Sí, señorita.**
    M: Yes, Miss.

13. **J: Tráigame una taza de café con leche y panecillos.**
    J: Bring me a cup of coffee and some rolls.

14. **P: Tráigame a mí lo mismo.**
    P: Bring me the same.

15. **J: Y usted, Luisa. ¿Qué va a comer?**
    J: And you, Louise? What are you going to eat?

16. **L: Yo como muy poco.**
    L: I don't eat very much.

17. **J: La línea. ¿No es así?**
    J: Your figure, I suppose?

18. **L: No precisamente . . . más que nada es mi costumbre.**
L: Not exactly—habit more than anything else.

19. **M: Usted me dirá, señorita.**
M: What will you have, Miss?

20. **L: Té con limón, galletas y un huevo pasado por agua.**
L: Tea and lemon, biscuits, and a soft-boiled egg.

21. **J: Mozo, ¿quiere usted traerme una servilleta?**
J: Waiter, would you please bring me a napkin?

22. **L: Y a mí me trae un tenedor, por favor.**
L: And a fork for me, please.

23. **P: Haga el favor de traernos un poco más de azúcar.**
P: Please bring us a little more sugar.

24. **J: Y después nos dará la cuenta . . . Ahí tiene, camarero, quédese con la vuelta.**
J: And then let's have a check. . . . Here you are, waiter. Keep the change.

25. **M: Muchas gracias, señor.**
M: Thank you, sir.

NOTES

1. *Tendrás, lit.,* "you will have." This is the future familiar singular form used to people you know well. See p. 31 for the difference between the familiar and polite forms.

2. "Yes, I have."

3. *Tengo una hambre canina.* I'm hungry as a wolf ("as a dog"). *Canino* canine (from *can* dog). The common word for "dog" is *perro*. *Tengo* (I have) is from *tener* to have (see p. 191).

4. *Camarero* waiter. Another word for "waiter" is *mozo*.

5. *Díganme los señores.* "Let the gentlemen tell me." *Digan* (they say) is from *decir* to say (see p. 191).

6. *Queremos* we would like; from *querer* to want, like (see p. 193).

7. *Podría* could you; from *poder* to be able (see p. 284). *Servirnos* to serve us. Notice that the *nos* ("us") is added directly to *servir* (see p. 257).

9. *¿Con qué lo sirven?* What do you serve with it? *Desayuno* is a light breakfast consisting usually of coffee and rolls, or else chocolate with biscuits or coffee cake. The regular restaurants don't usually serve breakfast; only hotels and cafés do.

10. *Panecillos* rolls

16. "I eat very little."

17. "Your figure, isn't it?" *Línea* line; here it means "figure." *Guardar la línea* to keep one's figure.

18. "More than anything else it's my habit." *Costumbre* habit; custom.

19. *Decir* to say. *Usted me dirá, señorita* ("You will say.") What will you have, Miss? Other uses of *Usted dirá*: *Sírvame un poco de cognac.—Usted dirá.* May I have a little brandy.—Say when. *Tengo algo que decirle—Usted dirá.* I have something to tell you.—Go ahead. *¿Le prestamos el dinero?—Usted dirá.* Shall we lend him the money?—It's up to you to say. You decide.

20. *Huevo* egg. *Un par de huevos fritos* two fried eggs. *Huevos pasados por agua* soft-boiled eggs. *Huevos revueltos* scrambled eggs.

22. "And to me bring a fork."

23. "Do the favor to bring us a little more (of) sugar."

24. "And then you will give us the check." *Dará* you will give; from *dar* to give (see p. 190). *Quedar* to remain, stay. *Se quedó en casa.* He stayed at home. *Quedar* is often used where we use the verb "to be": *¿Dónde queda el hotel?* Where is the hotel? *Quedarse con algo* to keep something.—Another word for "change" is *cambio.*

QUIZ 32

1. _____ (we want) *desayuno para tres personas.*
   a. *queremos*
   b. *desayunar*
   c. *apetito*

2. *¿*_____ (is there) *mantequilla?*
   a. *sirven*
   b. *hay*
   c. *podría*

3. *Tráigame a mi lo* _____ (same).
   a. *muy*
   b. *mismo*
   c. *espere*

4. *¿Qué va a* _____ (eat)?
   a. *sirven*
   b. *poco*
   c. *comer*

5. *Yo como muy* _____ (little).
   a. *va*
   b. *esto*
   c. *poco*

6. *Quiere usted* _____ (bring me) *una servilleta.*
   a. *costumbre*
   b. *traerme*
   c. *dirá*

7. _____ (afterwards) *nos dará la cuenta.*
   a. *favor*
   b. *tenedor*
   c. *después*

ANSWERS

1 a; 2 b; 3 b; 4 c; 5 c; 6 b; 7 c.

65. A SAMPLE MENU

MENÚ	MENU
Entremeses variados	Hors d'oeuvres
Sopa de fideos	Noodle soup
Puré de guisantes	Pea soup
Tortilla de cebolla	Onion omelet
Arroz con pollo	Chicken and rice
Pollo asado	Roast chicken
Cordero asado	Roast lamb
Bistec con patatas	Steak with French-fried
Ensalada de lechuga	potatoes
con tomate	Lettuce and tomato salad
Queso y fruta	Cheese and fruit
Café	Coffee

LESSON 36

66. A LA BUSCA DE PISO
APARTMENT HUNTING

(Apartment Hunting)

1. **Vengo a ver el piso.**
   I've come to see ("I come to see") the apartment.

2. **¿Cuál de ellos?**
   Which one?

3. **El que está por alquilar.**
   The one which is for rent.

4. **Hay dos.**
   There are two.

5. **¿Puede usted darme algún detalle de los pisos?**
   Can you describe them?

6. **El del quinto piso es sin muebles.**
   The one on the fifth floor is unfurnished.

7. **¿Y el otro?**
   And the other one?

8. **El del segundo piso es amueblado.**
   The one on the second floor is furnished.

9. **¿Cuántas habitaciones tienen?**
   How many rooms do they have?

10. **El del quinto tiene cuatro habitaciones, cocina y baño.**
    The one on the fifth floor has four rooms, a kitchen and a bath.

11. **¿Da a la calle?**
    Does it face the street?

12. **No, da al patio.**
    No, it faces a court.

13. **¿Cómo es el del segundo piso?**
    And the one on the second floor?

14. **El del segundo tiene un dormitorio, sala y comedor.**
    The one on the second floor has a bedroom, a living room and a dining room.

15. **¿Da también al patio?**
    Does it also face out on a court?

16. **No, da a la calle.**
    No, it faces the street.

17. **¿Cuánto es el alquiler?**
    How much is the rent?

18. **El alquiler del más grande es cinco mil pesetas al año, además del agua y el gas.**
The larger one is five thousand pesetas a year, plus water and gas.

19. **¿Y el amueblado?**
And the furnished one?

20. **Este cuesta siete mil pesetas al año, todo incluído.**
That one costs seven thousand pesetas a year, everything included.

21. **¿Qué clase de muebles tiene? ¿Están los muebles en buen estado?**
What kind of furniture does it have? Is the furniture in good condition?

22. **Los muebles son modernos y están en magníficas condiciones.**
It's modern furniture and it's in excellent condition.

23. **¿Están incluídos la ropa de cama y el servicio de mesa?**
Are linen and silverware included?

24. **Usted hallará todo lo que necesite, incluso un juego de utensilios de cocina.**
You'll find everything you need, even a complete set of kitchen utensils.

25. **¿Hay que firmar un contrato?**
Does one have to sign a lease?

26. **Para eso usted tendrá que ver al administrador.**
You'll have to see the renting agent for that.

27. **¿Cuáles son las condiciones?**
What are the terms?

28. **Un mes adelantado y otro de fianza.**
One month's rent in advance and another month's rent as a deposit.

29. **¿Es eso todo?**
Is that all?

30. **Por supuesto, usted tendrá que dar referencias.**
Of course, you'll have to give references.

31. **A propósito, ¿hay ascensor?**
By the way, is there an elevator?

32. **No, no hay ascensor.**
No, there isn't any elevator.

33. **¡Qué lástima!**
That's too bad.

34. **Aparte de esto la casa es muy moderna.**
Aside from that, the house is very modern.

35. **¿Qué quiere usted decir?**
What do you mean?

36. **Hay calefacción central y escalera de servicio.**
There's central heating and a back stairway.

37. **¿Hay agua caliente?**
Is there any hot water?

38. **Por supuesto. Los cuartos de baño han sido reformados recientemente.**
Of course. The bathrooms were recently remodeled.

39. **Ah, se me olvidaba... ¿Hay cuartos para las criadas?**
Oh, I forgot—are there servants' quarters?

40. **Sí, y muy buenos.**
Yes, ("and") very good ones.

41. **¿Se pueden ver los pisos?**
    Can one see the apartments?

42. **Unicamente por las mañanas.**
    Only in the morning.

43. **Muy bien. Vendré mañana por la mañana.
    Muchas gracias.**
    Very well, I'll come tomorrow morning.
    Thanks a lot.

44. **De nada. Servidor de usted.**
    Not at all. Glad to be able to help you ("at your
    service").

NOTES

Title: *A la busca de piso.* In search of an apartment.

1. *Piso* apartment, floor. Another word for "apartment" widely used throughout Spanish America
   is *apartamento.* It is also called *cuarto* in Madrid and in other cities in Spain. Apartments to
   let are usually indicated by a sign hung in the
   middle of the window or balcony; if hung to the
   side it means that there are single rooms to let.

2. "Which of them?"

3. *Alquilar* to let, to lease, to rent, to hire.

5. "Can you give me some details about the apartments?"

6. *Sin muebles* ("without furniture") unfurnished.
   You can also say *No amueblado* or *sin
   amueblar. Muebles* furniture. *Amueblar* to fur-
   nish.

8. *Principal* (main, principal) is the first floor in
   Spain. *Los cuartos del principal* the apartments
   on the first floor. *Piso bajo* or *planta baja*
   ground floor. *El primer piso* (the first floor) in
   Spain usually corresponds to the second or third

floor in the United States. In Spanish America, however, floors are generally counted the way they are in the United States; for example, *el piso primero* in Mexico City corresponds to our "first floor."

9. Other words for "room" are *cuarto* and *pieza*.

11. *Da a la calle*. It faces the street. It overlooks the street. *Da* is from *dar* to give (see p. 190).

14. *Dormitorio* bedroom. You can also say *alcoba* and *cuarto de dormir*. *Comedor* dining room. *Baño* bath. *Cuarto de baño* bathroom. *Cocina* kitchen.

20. *Cuesta* costs; from *costar* to cost (see p. 268).

21. Notice that the word for "furniture" *(los muebles)* is plural. *Estado* state, condition.

23. *Ropa de cama* ("bed linen") sheets and pillowcases. *Servicio de mesa* table service (silverware, plates, cups, glasses, tablecloth, napkins, etc.).

24. *Hallará* you will find. For the future tense (see p. 266.)

25. *Contrato* contract, agreement, lease. *Contrato de arriendo* or *contrato* lease.

27. *Cuáles* is the plural of *cuál* what, which. It is plural here because it modifies *las condiciones*, which is plural.

28. *Un mes adelantado y otro de fianza* one month in advance and one month's deposit. *Adelantado* or *por adelantado* in advance. *Fianza* guarantee, bond, security, bail. It's customary in Spain to leave a month's rent as a deposit and to pay a month's rent in advance.

35. *¿Qué quiere usted decir?* What do you mean?

38. *Reformados* (remodeled) is masculine plural because it refers to *los cuartos*. *Buenos* (good) is also masculine plural for the same reason.

39. *Se me olvidaba*. I forgot.

QUIZ 33

1. _____ (I come) *a ver el piso.*
   a. *viene*
   b. *vengo*
   c. *esta*

2. *El que* _____ (is) *por alquilar.*
   a. *ver*
   b. *ellos*
   c. *está*

3. _____ (there are) *dos.*
   a. *hay*
   b. *vengo*
   c. *es*

4. *Es* _____ (without) *muebles.*
   a. *quinto*
   b. *otro*
   c. *sin*

5. ¿_____ (how) *están dispuestas las habitaciones?*
   a. *cuánto*
   b. *cómo*
   c. *de*

6. ¿*Da a la* _____ (street)?
   a. *patio*
   b. *sala*
   c. *calle*

7. *Da* _____ (also) *al patio.*
   a. *también*
   b. *otro*
   c. *calle*

8. *Este* _____ (costs) *siete mil pesetas.*
   a. *cuesta*
   b. *todo*
   c. *cuanto*

9. *Usted* _____ (will find) *todo.*
   a. *necesite*
   b. *firmar*
   c. *hallará*

10. *La casa es* _____ (very) *moderna.*
    a. *esto*
    b. *muy*
    c. *que*

ANSWERS

1 b; 2 c; 3 a; 4 c; 5 b; 6 c; 7 a; 8 a; 9 c; 10 b.

67. SOME COMMON VERBS

1. *Tener* "to have"

   a. I have

tengo	*tenemos*
tienes	*tenéis*
tiene	*tienen*

Tengo esto.	I have this. I've got this.
No tengo nada.	I don't have anything.
¿Lo tiene usted?	Do you have it?
No lo tengo.	I don't have it.
Tengo tiempo.	I have time.
No tengo dinero.	I haven't any money.
No tengo tiempo.	I haven't any time.
No tiene amigos.	He hasn't any friends.
Tengo hambre.	I'm hungry.
Tengo sed.	I'm thirsty.
Tengo sueño.	I'm sleepy.
Tengo frío.	I'm cold.
Tengo calor.	I'm warm.
Tengo razón.	I'm right.
No tiene razón.	He's not right

No tienen razón.	They're wrong.
¿Tiene usted amigos en Madrid?	Do you have (any) friends in Madrid?
No tengo amigos en Madrid.	I don't have any friends in Madrid.
¿Tiene usted un cigarrillo?	Do you have a cigarette?
No tengo cigarrillos.	I don't have any cigarettes.
¿Tiene usted lumbre?	Do you have a light?
No tengo cerillas.	I don't have matches.
Tengo veinte años.	I'm twenty.
Tengo dolor de cabeza.	I have a headache.
Tengo dolor de muelas.	I have a toothache.
¿Qué tiene usted?	What's the matter with you?
No tengo nada.	Nothing's the matter with me.
¿Cuánto dinero tiene usted?	How much money do you have?
No tengo nada de dinero.	I haven't any money at all.
Tengo necesidad de . . .	I need . . .
Tengo necesidad de eso.	I need that.

b. *Tener que* translates "to have to":

Tengo que ir.	I have to go. I must go.
Tengo que irme.	I have to leave.
Tengo que escribir una carta.	I have to write a letter.
Tengo mucho que hacer.	I have a lot to do.

c. Do I Have It?

¿Lo tengo yo?	Do I have it?
¿Lo tienes tú?	Do you have it?

¿Lo tiene él?	Does he have it?
¿Lo tiene ella?	Does she have it?
¿Lo tenemos nosotros?	Do we have it?
¿Lo tenéis vosotros?	Do you have it?
¿Lo tienen ellos?	Do they have it?

d. Don't I Have It?

¿No lo tengo yo?	Don't I have it?
¿No lo tienes tú?	Don't you have it?
¿No lo tiene él?	Doesn't he have it?
¿No lo tiene ella?	Doesn't she have it?
¿No lo tenemos nosotros?	Don't we have it?
¿No lo tenéis vosotros?	Don't you have it?
¿No lo tienen ellos?	Don't they have it?

QUIZ 34

1. *No tengo dinero.*	1. I have a headache.
2. *No tengo nada.*	2. Don't you have it?
3. *No tiene razón.*	3. I don't have it.
4. *Tengo sueño.*	4. I'm cold.
5. *¿Lo tiene él?*	5. I'm warm.
6. *No lo tengo.*	6. I don't have any money.
7. *Tengo hambre.*	7. Does he have it?
8. *Tengo frío.*	8. He's not right.
9. *Tengo veinte años.*	9. I'm thirsty.
10. *¿No lo tienes tú?*	10. I have a lot to do.
11. *Tengo que irme.*	11. I don't have anything.
12. *Tengo calor.*	12. I'm sleepy.
13. *Tengo sed.*	13. I'm hungry.
14. *Tengo dolor de cabeza.*	14. I have to leave.
15. *Tengo mucho que hacer.*	15. I'm twenty years old.

ANSWERS

1—6; 2—11; 3—8; 4—12; 5—7; 6—3; 7—13; 8—4;
9—15; 10—2; 11—14; 12—5; 13—9; 14—1; 15—10.

2. *Haber* "to have" *(auxiliary)*

he	hemos
has	habéis
ha	han

a. *Haber* never means "to have" in the sense of "to possess" (*tener* is used in this sense). It is used with the past participle to form compound tenses:

He aprendido el español en México.	I learned Spanish in Mexico.
He pasado una semana en Cuba.	I spent a week in Cuba.
¿Has escrito la carta?	Have you written the letter?
¿Ha venido su hermano?	Has your brother come?

b. *Haber* is used in expressions of time and weather:

¿Cuánto ha?	How long ago?
Tres horas ha.	Three hours ago.
Poco ha.	A little while ago.
Años ha.	Years ago.
Hay niebla.	It's foggy. ("There is fog.")
Hay humedad.	It's humid. ("There is humidity.")

c. The third person singular *hay* means "there is" or "there are":

Hay mucha gente aquí.	There are a lot of people here.

Hubo and *Había* (see p. 283) means "there was" or "there were":

Hubo un incendio.	There was a fire.
Había una casa allí.	There was a house there.
Hubo mucha gente.	There were many people.

Habrá (see p. 283) means "there will be":

Habrá mucha gente.	There will be many people.

d. *Haber de* means "to have to":

Ha de hacerlo.	He has to do it.
He de ir al centro.	I have to go downtown.
Ha de venir mañana.	She has to come tomorrow.

e. *Hay que* means "it is necessary," "one has to," "one must":

Hay que aprender los verbos.	One must ("it is necessary to") learn the verbs.
Hay que dar vuelta a la derecha.	It's necessary to (you must, one must) turn ("given a turn") to the right.

3. *Hacer* "to do," "make"

hago	hacemos
haces	hacéis
hace	hacen

¿Cuánto tiempo le tomará para hacer esto?	How long will it take you to make (do) that?
¿Cómo se hace esto?	How do you make (do) this?
¿Qué haces?	What are you making (doing)?

¿Me puede enseñar cómo hacer esto?	Can you show me how to do this?

a. The third person singular of *hacer* is used in expressions about the weather:

Hace (muy) buen tiempo.	The weather's nice. ("It's good weather.")
Hace (muy) mal tiempo.	The weather's bad. ("It's bad weather.")
Hace (mucho) frío.	It's (very) cold.
Hacía (mucho) calor.	It was (very) warm (hot).
Ha hecho (mucho) sol.	It's been (very) sunny.

b. *Hace* often translates "ago":

Hace tres años.	Three years ago.
Hace seis meses.	Six months ago.
Se lo dije hace tres semanas.	I told it to him three weeks ago.

c. Notice the use of *hacer* in these expressions of time:

Hace dos horas que estudio.	I have been studying for two hours. ("It makes two hours that I study.")
Hace un año que está en Madrid.	He has been in Madrid for a year. ("It makes a year that he is in Madrid.")

QUIZ 35

1. Ha hecho sol.	1. Six months ago.
2. ¿Qué haces?	2. It's very cold.
3. Hace buen tiempo.	3. Three years ago.
4. Hace dos horas que estudio.	4. I told it to him three weeks ago.

5. *Hace un año que está en Madrid.*	5. What are you doing?
6. *Hace mucho frío.*	6. He has been in Madrid for a year.
7. *Hace tres años.*	7. It's been sunny.
8. *Se lo dije hace tres semanas.*	8. The weather is nice.
9. *¿Cómo se hace esto?*	9. I have been studying for two hours.
10. *Hace seis meses.*	10. How do you do this?

ANSWERS

1—7; 2—5; 3—8; 4—9; 5—6; 6—2; 7—3; 8—4; 9—10; 10—1.

LESSON 37

68. SOY FORASTERO
I'M A STRANGER HERE

(I'm A Stranger Here)

1. **Perdone usted.**
   Pardon me.

2. **¿En qué puedo servirle?**
   What can I do for you?

3. **¿Podría darme usted alguna información?**
   Could you give me some information?

4. **Con mucho gusto.**
   Gladly. ("With much pleasure.")

5. **No conozco la ciudad y no puedo orientarme.**
   I don't know this town and I can't find my way around.

6. **Pues, es muy sencillo.**
   Well, it's quite simple.

7. **Es que soy forastero.**
   You see, I'm a stranger here.

8. **En ese caso le enseñaré la ciudad.**
   In that case, I'll show you the town.

9. **Pues, se lo agradercería mucho.**
   I'd appreciate that a lot. ("Then, I'd be very grateful to you.")

10. **¿Ve ese edificio grande de la esquina?**
    Do you see that large building on the corner?

11. **¿Aquél de la bandera?**
    The one with the flag?

12. **Exactamente. Ese es el Correo. Frente a él, al otro lado de la calle . . .**
    That's right. ("Exactly.") That's the Post Office. Opposite it, on the other side of the street . . .

13. **¿Dónde?**
    Where?

14. **Allá. ¿Ve usted ese otro edificio con el reloj?**
    Over there. Do you see that other building with the clock?

15. **Ah sí, ya veo.**
    Oh, yes, now I see.

16. **Es el Ayuntamiento.**
    That's the City Hall.

17. **Ya veo . . . A propósito, ¿cómo se llama esta calle?**
    I see. . . . By the way, what's the name of this street?

18. **La calle Mayor.**
Main Street.

19. **¿Dónde está la Comisaría de Policía?**
Where is the Police Station?

20. **Al final de la calle. Siga usted todo derecho
. . .**
At the end of the street. Go straight ahead.

21. **¿Ya si la paso de largo?**
What if I miss it?

22. **No tiene pérdida. Es un edificio grande,
rodeado de una verja . . . ¿Ve usted esa
tienda?**
You can't miss it. It's a big building with an
iron fence around it ("surrounded by an iron
fence") . . . You see that store?

23. **¿Qué tienda? ¿La que está a la derecha?**
Which store? The one on the right? ("The one
which is on the right?")

24. **Exacto. Aquélla que tiene una bola verde en
el escaparate.**
Right, the one with a large green globe in the
window.

25. **¿Es una barbería?**
Is it a barber shop?

26. **No, es una farmacia. En la casa de al lado
hay un médico. Su nombre está en la puerta.**
No it's a pharmacy. The doctor lives right next
door. ("In the house to the side lives a doctor.") His name's on the door.

27. **¿Tiene la clínica en la misma casa en que vive?**
Does he have his office there as well? ("Does he have his office in the same house in which he lives?")

28. **Sí, pero se pasa las mañanas en el hospital.**
Yes, but he spends every morning at the hospital.

29. **¿Dónde está el hospital?**
Where's the hospital?

30. **El hospital está a dos cuadras de aquí, un poco antes de llegar a la carretera.**
The hospital is two blocks from here, just before ("a little before") you come to the main highway.

31. **¿Cómo puedo volver a mi hotel?**
How can I get back to my hotel?

32. **Vaya usted por aquí. Lo ve allí, junto al . . .**
Go this way. You see it there, next to the . . .

33. **. . . cine. ¿No es así?**
. . . movies. That's right, isn't it? ("isn't it so?")

34. **Exacto.**
Yes. ("Exact.")

35. **Ya me doy cuenta.**
Now I understand.

36. **¿Por qué no se compra usted una guía?**
Why don't you buy yourself a guidebook?

37. **No es mala idea. ¿Dónde podría comprar una?**
That's not a bad idea. Where can I buy one?

38. **En la estación o en cualquier kiosco de periódicos.**
In the station or at any newspaper stand.

39. **¿Está lejos la estación de aquí?**
Is the station far from here?

40. **La estación está al final del Paseo de las Delicias.**
The station is at the end of Delicias Avenue.

41. **¿Dónde hay un kiosco de periódicos por aquí?**
Where's there a newspaper stand near here?

42. **En la esquina tiene usted uno.**
There's one on this corner. ("On the corner you have one.")

43. **Le estoy muy agradecido.**
Thank you very much. ("I'm very grateful to you.")

44. **No tiene importancia. Me ha sido muy grato haberle sido útil.**
Not at all. ("It has no importance.") I'm very glad to have been of any help to you. ("I've been very glad to have been useful to you.")

45. **He tenido una gran suerte en haberle encontrado. Verdaderamente usted conoce muy bien la ciudad.**
I was certainly lucky to meet you. You really know this town very well.

46. **No es para menos. Soy el alcalde.**
It's not surprising. I'm the mayor.

NOTES

Title: *Soy forastero.* I'm a stranger.

1. *Perdone usted.* Pardon me. I beg your pardon. *Dispense usted.* Excuse me. *Hágame el favor...* ("Do me the favor...") Please... *Me hace el favor...* ("Do me the favor...")

Will you please... *¿Me hace el favor de decirme?* Will you please tell me? *Tenga la bondad* ("Have the goodness to...") Please ...*Sírvase decirme.* Please tell me. *¿Puede decirme?* Can you tell me? *Le agradecería que* ...I'd appreciate it if...*or* I'd be obliged to you if...

2. *Puedo.* I can; from *poder* to be able (see p. 195).

3. *¿Podría usted?* Could you?; from *poder* (see p. 284).

5. *Conozco.* I know; from *conocer* to know (see p. 276). *Orientarse* to orient oneself, to get one's bearings, to find one's way.

7. "It's that I'm a stranger." *Es que* the reason is that ...*or* It's because...

8. *Enseñar* to show, to teach.

9. *Se lo agradecería.* I would be grateful (see p. 254)

11. *Bandera* flag. Every public building in Spain has a flag mast and a coat of arms above the main entrance.

12. *Correo* mail. *El correo* the post office. *¿Dónde está el correo?* Where's the post office? Also *la casa de correos* and *la oficina de correos.* *¿A qué hora reparten el correo?* When is the mail distributed? At what time do they distribute the mail?

21. *Pasar de largo* to pass by without stopping, to pass by without noticing a place; to miss a place.

22. *Pérdida* loss. *No tiene pérdida.* ("It has no loss.") You can't miss it.

25. *Barbería* barber shop. Also *peluquería.*

27. *Tiene* he has; from *tener* to have (see p. 191). *Clínica* clinic; doctor's office. A "doctor's office" is also called *consultorio.*

30. *El hospital está a dos cuadras de aquí.* This is the expression used in Latin America. In Spain you say *El hospital está pasadas dos bocacalles.* ("The hospital is two street intersections passed.")

31. *Volver* to return.

35. *Doy* I give; from *dar* to give (see p. 190). *Cuenta* account; bill, check.

44. *Ha sido.* It has been; from *ser* (see p. 286).

45. *He tenido* I have had; from *tener.*

46. *No es para menos.* ("It's not for less."). It's no wonder. It's not surprising.—*Soy* I am; from *ser* (see p. 286).

QUIZ 36

1. *Es muy* _____ (simple).
   a. pues
   b. sencillo
   c. ciudad

2. *Le enseñaré la* _____ (city).
   a. caso
   b. ciudad
   c. orientar

3. *Ese edificio grande de la* _____ (corner).
   a. esquina
   b. calle
   c. correo

4. *Pues ése es el* _____ (post office).
   a. calle
   b. correo
   c. otro

5. ¿Ve usted esa _____ (store)?
   a. derecha
   b. tienda
   c. barbería

6. En la casa de al lado hay un _____ (doctor).
   a. médico
   b. farmacia
   c. nombre

7. Su nombre está en la _____ (door).
   a. misma
   b. puerta
   c. clínica

8. Tiene la clínica en la misma _____ (house)
   en que vive.
   a. puerta
   b. lado
   c. casa

9. Un poco _____ (before) de llegar a la
   carretera.
   a. después
   b. antes
   c. pasadas

10. ¿Dónde podría _____ (buy) una?
    a. comprar
    b. guía
    c. estación

ANSWERS
1 b; 2 b; 3 a; 4 b; 5 b; 6 a; 7 b; 8 c; 9 b; 10 a.

LESSON 38

69. SALUDANDO A UN VIEJO AMIGO
GREETING AN OLD FRIEND

(Meeting An Old Friend)

1. **P[1]: ¿Dónde está el señor Villanueva? ... El señor que acaba de llegar.**
   P: Where is Mr. Villanueva?—the gentleman who just arrived.

2. **G: Acaba de entrar en el comedor, señor García.**
   G: He's just gone into the dining room, Mr. Garcia.

3. **P:** *(entrando en el comedor y mirando a un lado y a otro):* **¡Ah! ¡Estás ahí! ¿Cómo estás, mi querido Juan?**
   P: *(entering the dining room and looking around)*: Oh, there you are! How are you, ("my dear") John?

4. **J: ¿Y tú, Pedro? ¿Estás bien?**
   J: How are you, Peter? ("And you, Peter, you're well?")

5. **P: ¿Buena travesía?**
   P: Did you have a good crossing?

6. **J: ¡Estupenda!**
   J: Wonderful!

7. **P: Mira. Voy a presentarte a mi esposa.**
   P: ("Look.") I'd like you to meet my wife.

8. **J: Me será un gran placer conocerla.**
   J: I'd be delighted to meet her.

---

[1]*P:* stands here for *Pedro* "Peter"; *G.* for *el gerente de hotel* "the hotel manager"; *J.* for *Juan* "John"; *M.* for *María* "Mary."

9. **P: María, te presento a mi viejo amigo, Juan Villanueva.**
   P: Mary, this is an old friend, John Villanueva.

10. **J: Encantado de conocerla, señora.**
    J: I'm very happy to know you.

11. **M: Y yo encantada también de conocerlo.**
    M: Glad to know you.

12. **J: Usted sabe que Pedro y yo somos viejos amigos.**
    J: You know that Peter and I are old friends.

13. **M: ¡Oh, ya lo sé! No hay día que no me hable de usted.**
    M: Oh, I know that. Not a day has gone by that he hasn't spoken about you. ("There has not been a day that he hasn't spoken about you.")

14. **J: ¿De verdad?**
    J: Really?

15. **P: No sabes la alegría que tengo de volverte a ver.**
    P: You don't know how happy it makes me to see you again.

16. **J: Yo también. ¡No has cambiado nada, Pedro!**
    J: The same here. You haven't changed a bit, Peter.

17. **P: Tú tampoco has cambiado nada. Estás tan joven como siempre.**
    P: You haven't changed either. You still look as young as ever.

18. **M: ¿Y le gustan a su esposa los Estados Unidos?**
    M: How does your wife like the United States?

19. **J: Ya está aclimatada.**
J: She's gotten completely used to it.

20. **M: Tengo entendido que la vida de Nueva York es distinta a la de Madrid.**
M: I understand that life in New York is different from life in Madrid.

21. **J: En efecto, hay muchas cosas allí que son diferentes.**
J: It certainly is. Many things there are different.

22. **M: ¿Por ejemplo?**
M: For example?

23. **J: Por ejemplo, no se le ocurriría a usted ir a desayunarse en una farmacia, ¿verdad?**
J: For example, you wouldn't think of going to a pharmacy for breakfast, would you?

24. **M: ¿En una farmacia?**
M: A pharmacy?

25. **P: ¿Qué broma es ésa?**
P: What kind of joke is that?

26. **J: No es broma. Estoy hablando en serio. Uno puede desayunarse en una farmacia ... o comer ... o cenar ...**
J: It's not a joke at all. I'm serious. One can have breakfast in a pharmacy or lunch or dinner. ...

27. **P: Por favor, no nos tomes el pelo.**
P: You're joking.

28. **M: Pero aquí, como usted sabe, en la farmacia sólo sirven las recetas médicas y venden medicinas.**
M: But here, as you know, ("in a pharmacy") they only fill prescriptions and sell medicine.

29. **J: Pues allí, además de recetas, sirven muy buena comida. Sobre todo helados y refrescos.**
J: Well, over there, in addition to the prescriptions, you can have a good meal, especially ice cream and refreshments.

30. **M: ¿Y comerá usted oliendo medicinas?**
M: And you eat with the smell of medicines around you?

31. **J: Nada, nada de eso. Son establecimientos grandes y muy bien organizados, refrigerados en verano y con calefacción en invierno. Y allí, repito, se puede comer como en un restaurant caulquiera.**
J: Oh no, nothing of the sort. They are large and well-organized establishments, air-cooled during the summer and heated during the winter. And there, I repeat, you can eat as well as in any restaurant.

32. **P: ¡En una farmacia! Hombre, por Dios, no me hagas reír.**
P: In a pharmacy! (''Man, for goodness' sake'') don't make me laugh!

33. **J: Sí, hombre, sí, en una farmacia. Pero allí la farmacia no lleva ese nombre. Se llama ''drug store.''**
J: Yes (''yes, man, yes''), in a pharmacy. But it's not called a pharmacy there; it's called a ''drugstore.''

34. **P: Yo veo el truco. Es farmacia pero no se llama farmacia. Entonces, si no se llama farmacia no es farmacia.**
P: Oh! I see the trick! It's a pharmacy but they don't call it a pharmacy. Then, if it's not called a pharmacy it's not a pharmacy.

35. **J: Pues bien, en un "drug store" hay sellos de correos, cigarros, cigarrillos, papel para cartas, aparatos eléctricos, juguetes, libros ...**

    J: Well then, in a drugstore you can get stamps, cigars, cigarettes, writing paper, electrical appliances, toys, books ...

36. **P: Entonces es un bazar.**

    P: Then it's a bazaar!

37. **J: Que no, hombre, que no, es un "drug store."**

    J: No, it's still a "drugstore." ("But no, man, no—it's a drugstore.")

38. **P: ¡Maravillas de los Estados Unidos!**

    P: The wonders of America!

NOTES

8. "It will be a great pleasure for me to know her."

9. "I'd like to introduce you to ..."

10. *Encantado de conocerla.* "Delighted to know you." *La* is used when addressing a woman. Speaking to a man you say *Encantado de conocerle.*

11. "And I'm also delighted to know you." *Y* and Notice that many Spanish sentences (see sentence 18) begin with *y.* In most cases this "and" can't be translated.

15. "You don't know the happiness I have. . . ."

16. "I also."

17. "You also have not changed at all."

18. *Le gustan a su esposa* does your wife like (see p. 127).

19. *Aclimatado* acclimated; used to. The feminine form *(aclimatada)* is used here because it refers to a woman.

23. "It would not occur to you to have breakfast in a pharmacy, would it?" *Ocurriría* it would occur (see p. 254). *Verdad* here means "would it?" (see p. 99).

26. *Estoy hablando* I'm speaking. (see p. 266). *En serio* in (all) seriousness.

27. *Tomar* to take. *El pelo* the hair. *No nos tomes el pelo.* ("Don't take our hair.") Don't make fun of us! Don't tease (kid) us!

30. "And you will eat smelling medicines?"

31. *Pedirá* you will ask for; from *pedir* to ask for, to seek (see p. 271).

33. *Hagas* you *(fam.)* make; from *hacer* to make (see p. 284).

34. *Llevar* to carry. *Llevar un nombre* ("to bear a name") to be named. *Llamarse* to be called, to be named.

35. *Papel para cartas* ("paper for letters") letter paper, stationery.

37. "But no, man, no—it's a drugstore."

QUIZ 37

1. ¿_____ (where) *está el señor Villanueva?*
   a. *cómo*
   b. *dónde*
   c. *entrar*

2. *El señor que acaba de* _____ (arrive).
   a. *llegar*
   b. *comedor*
   c. *lado*

3. *Voy a* _____ (introduce you) *a mi esposa.*
   a. *estupenda*
   b. *conocerla*
   c. *presentarte*

4. *Me será un gran placer* _____ (to know her).
   a. *esposa*
   b. *querido*
   c. *conocerla*

5. *Te presento a mi viejo* _____ (friend) *Julián.*
   a. *gran*
   b. *también*
   c. *amigo*

6. *Usted* _____ (know) *que somos viejos amigos.*
   a. *conocer*
   b. *sabe*
   c. *señora*

7. *Ya lo* _____ (I know).
   a. *sé*
   b. *viejos*
   c. *somos*

8. *No has* _____ (changed).
   a. *alegría*
   b. *cambiado*
   c. *volverte*

9. *Estás tan* _____ (young) *como siempre.*
   a. *joven*
   b. *nada*
   c. *día*

10. *La* _____ (life) *de Nueva York es distinta a la de Madrid.*
    a. *cosa*
    b. *vida*
    c. *calle*

11. *Hay muchas* _____ (things) *que son diferentes.*
    a. *vida*
    b. *allí*
    c. *cosas*

12. *Aquí* _____ (they sell) *medicinas.*
    a. sirven
    b. venden
    c. cenar

13. *Sirven muy* _____ (good) *comida.*
    a. buena
    b. pelo
    c. recetas

14. *Son establecimientos* _____ (large).
    a. sentido
    b. grandes
    c. salsa

15. *Refrigerados en* _____ (summer).
    a. repito
    b. verano
    c. nada

16. *Con calefacción en* _____ (winter).
    a. invierno
    b. repito
    c. como

17. *Allí se puede* _____ (eat).
    a. serio
    b. comer
    c. lleva

18. *La farmacia no lleva ese* _____ (name).
    a. llama
    b. puede
    c. nombre

19. *No me hagas* _____ (laugh).
    a. pero
    b. reír
    c. nombre

20. *En un "drug store" hay* _____ (books).
    a. *juguetes*
    b. *libros*
    c. *cartas*

ANSWERS

1 b.; 2 a.; 3 c.; 4 c.; 5 c.; 6 b.; 7 a.; 8 b.; 9 a.; 10 b.;
11 c.; 12 b.; 13 a.; 14 b.; 15 b.; 16 a.; 17 b.; 18 c.;
19 b.; 20 b.

70. THE COMMONEST VERBS AND THEIR COMMONEST FORMS

1. *Hacer* "to do," "make"

PRESENT	PAST	FUTURE	
hago	hice	haré	
haces	hiciste	harás	
hace	hizo	hará	IMPERATIVE
			¡Haz! (fam.)
hacemos	hicimos	haremos	¡Haced!
hacéis	hicisteis	haréis	
hacen	hicieron	harán	

Lo hice yo mismo.	I made (did) it myself.
Harán siempre lo que se les mande.	They'll always do what they're told.
Haré lo posible por ir.	I'll do my best to go.
Hazlo lo más pronto posible.	Do it as soon as possible.

2. *Haber* "to have" *(auxiliary)*

PRESENT	PAST	FUTURE	
he	hube	habré	
has	hubiste	habrás	
ha	hubo	habrá	IMPERATIVE
			¡He!
hemos	hubimos	habremos	¡Habed!
habéis	hubisteis	habréis	
han	hubieron	habrán	

He tratado de comunicarme con él, pero ha sido imposible.	I tried to get in touch with him but it was impossible.
He aquí los libros que me prestaste.	Here are the books you lent me.
¿Has ido alguna vez a la ópera?	Have you ever been to the opera?
Han ido varias veces a su casa.	They've been to his house several times.
Hubo mucha gente en la fiesta.	There were a lot of people at the party.
Habrá que ir mañana otra vez.	We'll have to go again tomorrow.

3. *Ir* "to go"

PRESENT	PAST	FUTURE	
voy	fuí	iré	
vas	fuiste	irás	
va	fué	irá	IMPERATIVE
			¡Ve!
vamos	fuimos	iremos	¡Id!
váis	fuisteis	iréis	
van	fueron	irán	

Voy a ir a Sud América el año que viene.	I'm going to go to South America next year.
El va a ir sin usted.	He's going to go without you.
Fuí a verle ayer.	I went to see him yesterday.
Iré a visitarles mañana.	I'll go to visit them tomorrow.
Vete pronto.	Go quickly.
¿Fuiste ayer al cine?	Did you go to the movies yesterday?
¡Vamos!	Let's go!
Anoche fuimos al teatro.	We went to the theater last night.

4. *Venir* "to come"

PRESENT	PAST	FUTURE	
vengo	*vine*	*vendré*	
vienes	*viniste*	*vendrás*	
viene	*vino*	*vendrá*	IMPERATIVE
			¡Ven!
venimos	*vinimos*	*vendremos*	*¡Venid!*
venís	*vinisteis*	*vendréis*	
vienen	*vinieron*	*vendrán*	

Tú vienes conmigo, ¿verdad?	You're coming with me, aren't you?
El siempre viene a mi casa.	He always comes to my house.
¿Cuándo viene ella?	When will she come?
Ellos vienen a menudo a la ciudad.	They come to the city often.
Ellos vienen a vernos mañana.	They're coming to see us tomorrow.

| *Vendrán a vernos esta tarde.* | They'll come to see us this afternoon. |
| *Ven a esta misma hora mañana.* | Come about this time tomorrow. |

5. *Andar* "to walk," "go"

PRESENT	PAST	FUTURE	
ando	*anduve*	*andaré*	
andas	*anduviste*	*andarás*	
anda	*anduvo*	*andará*	IMPERATIVE
			¡Anda!
andamos	*anduvimos*	*andaremos*	*¡Andad!*
andáis	*anduvisteis*	*andaréis*	
andan	*anduvieron*	*andarán*	

Anduve a pie todo el camino.	I walked all the way.
Andaremos juntos.	We'll walk together.
Anda más de prisa.	Walk faster.

6. *Dar* "to give"

PRESENT	PAST	FUTURE	
doy	*dí*	*daré*	
das	*diste*	*darás*	
da	*dió*	*dará*	IMPERATIVE
			¡Da!
damos	*dimos*	*daremos*	*¡Dad!*
dáis	*disteis*	*daréis*	
dan	*dieron*	*darán*	

¿Puede usted dármelo mañana?	Can you give it to me tomorrow?
Se lo dí ayer.	I gave it to him yesterday.
Daré lo que pueda.	I'll give what I can.

7. *Tener* "to have," "to hold"

PRESENT	PAST	FUTURE	
tengo	*tuve*	*tendré*	
tienes	*tuviste*	*tendrás*	
tiene	*tuvo*	*tendrá*	IMPERATIVE
			¡Ten!
tenemos	*tuvimos*	*tendremos*	*¡Tened!*
tenéis	*tuvisteis*	*tendréis*	
tienen	*tuvieron*	*tendrán*	

No tengo tiempo.	I haven't any time.
Usted tiene que conseguirlo cuanto antes.	You have to get it as soon as possible.
Tenemos visitas en casa.	We have guests at home.
Tuvo que salir temprano hoy.	He had to go out early today.
¿Tendrá usted tiempo?	Will you have time?
Tengo que ir a un concierto esta noche.	I have to go to a concert tonight.

8. *Decir* "to say"

PRESENT	PAST	FUTURE	
digo	*dije*	*diré*	
dices	*dijiste*	*dirás*	
dice	*dijo*	*dirá*	IMPERATIVE
			¡Dí!
decimos	*dijimos*	*diremos*	*¡Decid!*
decís	*dijisteis*	*diréis*	
dicen	*dijeron*	*dirán*	

El dijo que se iba.	He said he was leaving.
Ella dice que vendrá mañana.	She says she'll come tomorrow.
Ellos nunca dicen nada.	They never say anything.

Siempre dice lo que piensa.	He always says what he thinks.
Dí lo que quieras.	Say whatever you like.
¿Qué piensa usted que dirá?	What do you think he'll say?

9. *Poner* "to put"

PRESENT	PAST	FUTURE	
pongo	puse	pondré	
pones	pusiste	pondrás	
pone	puso	pondrá	IMPERATIVE
			¡Pon!
ponemos	pusimos	pondremos	¡Poned!
ponéis	pusisteis	pondréis	
ponen	pusieron	pondrán	

Lo puse sobre la mesa.	I put it on the table.
¿Dónde lo vas a poner?	Where are you going to put it?
Pon las cosas en su lugar.	Put everything in its place.
Poned la mesa cerca de la ventana.	Put the table near the window.

10. *Ponerse* "to put"

PRESENT	PAST	FUTURE
me pongo	me puse	me pondré
te pones	te pusiste	te pondrás
se pone	se puso	se pondrá
nos ponemos	nos pusimos	nos pondremos
os ponéis	os pusisteis	os pondréis
se ponen	se pusieron	se pondrán

Me puse tu sombrero por equivocación.	I put your hat on by mistake.
Ponte tu traje nuevo.	Put on your new suit.

Nos pusimos a jugar a las cartas.	We began to play cards.
El sol se pone a las cinco.	The sun sets at five.
Se pondrá furioso cuando lo sepa.	He'll be furious when he finds out.

11. *Querer* "to wish," "to want"

PRESENT	PAST	FUTURE	
quiero	*quise*	*querré*	
quieres	*quisiste*	*querrás*	
quiere	*quiso*	*querrá*	IMPERATIVE
			¡Quiere!
queremos	*quisimos*	*querremos*	*¡Quered!*
queréis	*quisisteis*	*querréis*	
quieren	*quisieron*	*querrán*	

Quiero ir.	I want to go.
La quiso mucho.	He loved her very much.
No querrá ir si no le acompañamos.	He won't go if we don't go with him.

12. *Traer* "to bring"

PRESENT	PAST	FUTURE	
traigo	*traje*	*traeré*	
traes	*trajiste*	*traerás*	
trae	*trajo*	*traerá*	IMPERATIVE
			¡Trae!
traemos	*trajimos*	*traeremos*	*¡Traed!*
traéis	*trajisteis*	*traeréis*	
traen	*trajeron*	*traerán*	

Se me olvidó traerlo.	I forgot to bring it.
Trae algún dinero contigo.	Bring some money with you.
Le trajo un regalo.	He brought her a present.

13. *Salir* "to leave"

PRESENT	PAST	FUTURE	
salgo	salí	saldré	
sales	saliste	saldrás	
sale	salió	saldrá	IMPERATIVE
			¡Sal!
salimos	salimos	saldremos	¡Salid!
salís	salisteis	saldréis	
salen	salieron	saldrán	

Salgo el miércoles.	I'm leaving on Wednesday.
Salió por aquí.	He went out this way.

14. *Ver* "to see"

PRESENT	PAST	FUTURE	
veo	ví	veré	
ves	viste	verás	
ve	vió	verá	IMPERATIVE
			¡Ve!
vemos	vimos	veremos	¡Ved!
véis	visteis	veréis	
ven	vieron	verán	

No ve bien sin sus anteojos.	He can't see well without his glasses.
Lo ví ayer.	I saw him yesterday.
Ya verás que lo que digo es verdad.	You'll see that what I say is true.

15. *Saber* "to know"

PRESENT	PAST	FUTURE	
sé	supe	sabré	IMPERATIVE
sabes	supiste	sabrás	¡Sabe!
sabe	supo	sabrá	¡Sabed!

PRESENT	PAST	FUTURE
sabemos	*supimos*	*sabremos*
sabéis	*supisteis*	*sabréis*
saben	*supieron*	*sabrán*

Sé que eso es cierto. — I know it's true.
¿Supiste la noticia? — Did you hear the news?
Ya lo sabrán a tiempo. — They'll find it out in time.

16. *Poder* "to be able"

PRESENT	PAST	FUTURE	
puedo	*pude*	*podré*	
puedes	*pudiste*	*podrás*	
puede	*pudo*	*podrá*	IMPERATIVE
			¡Puede!
podemos	*pudimos*	*podremos*	*¡Poded!*
podéis	*pudisteis*	*podréis*	
pueden	*pudieron*	*podrán*	

¿Dónde puedo mandar un telegrama? — Where can I send a telegram?
¿Podrás venir esta noche? — Will you be able to come tonight?

LESSON 39

71. WHAT'S IN A NAME?

(What's In A Name?)

¿Cómo se llama él?
What's his name?

Se llama José Sánchez.
His name is Jose Sanchez.

¿Cómo se llama la señorita que está con él?
What's the name of the young lady with him?

Se llama María Suárez Navarro.
Her name is Maria Suarez Navarro.

¿Cómo se llama su padre?
What's her father's name?

Su padre se llama Antonio Suárez Coello.
Her father's name is Antonio Suarez Coello.

No me explico por qué ella se llama Navarro y su padre Coello.
I can't understand why her name is Navarro and her father's name is Coello.

Usted se equivoca. Ella no se llama Navarro, ni su padre Coello. Navarro y Coello son apellidos maternos, y no paternos.
You're wrong. Her name isn't Navarro and her father's isn't Coello. Navarro and Coello are maternal not paternal surnames.

Perdóneme usted pero no le entiendo. ¿Qué es eso de apellidos maternos y paternos?
Excuse me but I don't understand you. What do you mean by maternal and paternal surnames?

Se lo explicaré a usted. Toda persona en España y en Hispanoamérica usa dos apellidos: el paterno y el materno.
I'll explain it to you. Everyone in Spain and in Spanish America has two family names: the maternal and paternal.

¿Como es eso?
How come? ("How is this?")

**Por ejemplo, el nombre de pila de esa señorita es
María y sus apellidos son Suárez y Navarro.
Suárez por su padre y Navarro por su madre.
Así que ella se llama Señorita María Suárez
Navarro.**

For instance, the Christian ("baptismal") name of
that young lady is Maria and her family names are
Suarez and Navarro; Suarez for her father and
Navarro for her mother. So her name is Miss Maria
Suarez Navarro.

**Ahora me doy cuenta. No es correcto llamar a una
persona por su apellido materno.**

Now I see. It's wrong to call a person by his maternal
surname.

**Exacto. Usted la puede llamar Señorita María
Suárez Navarro o Señorita Suárez, pero nunca
Señorita Navarro.**

That's right. ("Exact.") You may call her Miss
Maria Suarez Navarro or Miss Suarez, but never
Miss Navarro.

¿Cómo se llama su madre?

What's her mother's name?

Su madre se llama Vicenta Navarro de Suárez.

Her mother's name is Vicenta Navarro de Suarez.

¿Por qué Navarro de Suárez?

Why Navarro de Suarez?

**Pues, porque Navarro es su apellido de soltera y
Suárez el de su marido.**

Because Navarro is her maiden name and Suarez her
husband's.

¿Cómo se dirige una carta a nombre de los dos?

How does one address a letter to them ("to the
two")?

Usted debería escribir en el sobre "Señores de Suárez Coello" o "Señor Don Antonio Suárez Coello y Señora."

You should write on the envelope "Mr. and Mrs. Suarez Coello" or "Mr. Antonio Suarez Coello and wife."

NOTES

This complicated system has one advantage: it eliminates the need for the equivalent of our "junior." For example, if *Antonio Suárez Coello* names his son *Antonio,* and the mother's name is *Navarro,* the son's name is *Antonio Suárez Navarro* and so there is no need for a word like "junior" or "the second" to keep father and son apart.

If one brother whose family name is *Suárez Navarro* marries *Señorita Ruiz González* and another brother marries *Señorita García Pérez,* and each had a son named *José,* the two cousins sign themselves *José Suárez Ruiz* and *José Suárez García.* Sometimes only the first letter of the mother's name is written: *José Suárez R.* and *José Suárez G.*

A married woman keeps her maiden name and adds *de* followed by her husband's family name: *Navarro de Suárez.* Thus if *Señorita María Suárez Navarro* marries *Señor Alberto Sánchez* her name becomes *Señora María Suárez de Sánches. De* ("of") before the husband's name stands for *esposa de* ("wife of").

LESSON 40

72. BRIGHTER SPANISH

(Brighter Spanish)

UNA PERDIDA DE POCA IMPORTANCIA
A Minor Loss

—Señora, hágame el favor de darme "La Libertad." No tengo suelto.[1]

¿Puede usted cambiarme este billete?

—Ya me lo pagará usted mañana—dice la vendedora.

—¿Y si yo me muriera esta noche?

—¡Bah! No sería muy grande la pérdida.

"Madam, please give me a copy of 'Liberty.' I haven't any change. Could you change this bill for me?"

"You can pay for it tomorrow," says the woman selling the newspaper.

"What if I should die tonight?"

"Oh, it wouldn't be a very great loss."

UNA LECCION DE ETIQUETA
A Lesson in Etiquette

Pedro y Juan van a comer a un restaurante. Los dos piden bistec. El camarero les sirve poco después. Pedro se apodera del bistec más grande. Juan, contrariado, le dice:

¡Qué mal educado eres! Has sido el primero en servirte y has cogido el trozo más grande.

---

[1] Notice how Spanish punctuation in dialogues differs from English: (1) There are no quotation marks and (2) each change of speaker is indicated by a dash (see p. 214)

Pedro responde:

—Estando tú en mi lugar, ¿qué pedazo hubieras cogido?

—El más pequeño, por supuesto.

—Entonces, ¿de qué te quejas? ¿No lo tienes ahí?

Peter and John go to a restaurant to eat. They both ask for steak. The waiter brings the steaks to them shortly afterwards. Peter grabs the larger steak. John says to him angrily:

"What bad manners you have! You helped yourself first and you took the larger piece."

Peter answers:

"If you had been in my place, which piece would you have taken?"

"The smaller, of course."

"Then what are you complaining about? You have it, haven't you?"

NOTES

Pérdida loss.

De poca importancia of little importance.

Hágame el favor. Please. ("Do me the favor.")

Dar to give; *darme* to give me.

¿Puede usted? Can you?; from *poder* to be able (see p. 195).

Cambiar to change; *cambiarme* to change for me.

Ya already. Here it makes the sentence more expressive.

Pagará you will pay; from *pagar* to pay.

Dice he (she) says; from *decir* to say (see p. 191).

Vendedor merchant, storekeeper; *vendedora* (woman) storekeeper.

Muriera should die; from *morir* to die.

Sería would be; from *ser* to be (see p. 286).

Esta noche ("this night") tonight.
Piden they ask for; from *pedir* to ask for.
Poco después a little afterwards, a little later.
Mal educado ill-bred.
Has cogido you *(fam.)* took; from *coger* to take.
Hubieras cogido would have taken.

UN OPTIMISTA
An Optimist

Mirando la solicitud, el jefe de una importante firma, abre los ojos con asombro cuando nota que el pretendiente al empleo, que carecía de experiencia, pide un sueldo excesivo.

—¿No le parece—preguntó azorado,—que usted pide demasiado sueldo para la poca experiencia que tiene?

—Por el contrario—replicó el aspirante,—un trabajo del que no se sabe absolutamente nada es más difícil y debe pagarse mejor.

The head of an important firm, looking at an application, is astonished when he notices that the applicant, though lacking experience, asks for an excessive salary.

Rather puzzled, he asks him: "Doesn't it seem to you that you're asking for an excessive salary considering the little experience you have?"

"On the contrary," replies the applicant. "Work performed by one who knows nothing about it is harder and should be better paid."

NOTES

Mirando looking; from *mirar* to look.
Abre opens; from *abrir* to open.

Los ojos the eyes.

Con asombro with astonishment.

Nota he notes; from *notar* to note, see.

Carecía he lacked; from *carecer* to lack.

Pide asks for; from *pedir* to ask for (see p. 271).

No le parece doesn't it seem to you; from *parecer* to seem.

Preguntó he asked; from *preguntar* to ask.

Demasiado too much.

Un sueldo a salary.

Replicó he replied; from *replicar* to reply, answer.

El que no sabe (the) one who doesn't know; from *saber* to know (see p. 285).

No saber nada not to know anything.

EL ESPIRITU PRACTICO
The Practical Mind

Un comerciante se presentó un día en casa de un campesino, pidiéndole que le procurase una libra de mantequilla. El campesino le contestó que se la daría a cambio de un par de calcetines de lana.

Cuando el comerciante se lo dijo a su mujer, ésta le dió la solución:

—Tenemos una colcha de lana—le dijo—, la desharé y haré un par de calcetines.

Así lo hizo, y el comerciante se llevó la libra de mantequilla, por la que dió el par de calcetines. Desde entonces, cuando el comerciante necesitaba mantequilla, su mujer deshacía un poco de la colcha y tejía unos calcetines. Pero llegó un día en que sólo tuvo lana para un calcetín. El comerciante se lo llevó al campesino, pidiéndole media libra de mantequilla.

—No—respondió el campesino—, le daré una libra. Mi mujer deshace los calcetines para una colcha que está casi terminando.

A merchant went to the house of a farmer and asked him if he could get him a pound of butter. The farmer said he would give it to him in exchange for a pair of woolen socks.

When the merchant told his wife about it, she suggested this solution: "We have a woolen quilt," she said. "I can unravel it and make a pair of socks."

She did so and the merchant got a pound of butter in exchange for the pair of socks. From then on, when the merchant needed butter, his wife unraveled some of the quilt and knitted socks. But one day there was just enough wool left to make one sock. The merchant took it to the farmer and asked him for half a pound of butter.

"No," said the farmer, "I'll give you a pound. My wife unravels the socks to make a quilt. All she needs is this one sock to finish it. . . . "

NOTES

El espíritu the spirit, mind.

Pidiéndole asking him: *pidiendo* asking; from *pedir* to ask; *le* him.

Procurase that he should get; from *procurar* to secure, get.

Daría that he would give; from *dar* to give.

Dijo he said, told; from *decir* to say, tell.

Dío he gave; from *dar* to give.

Desharé I will unravel; from *deshacer* to undo, unravel (*hacer* to do).

Hizo he did, made; from *hacer* to do, make.

Se llevó he carried or took away with him; from *llevarse* to carry or take away with one.

Llegó there came; from *llegar* to arrive.

Tuvo he had; from *tener* to have.

Daré I will give; from *dar* to give (see p. 283).

Que está casi terminando which she has almost finished. Or: *Mi mujer deshace los calcetines para hacer una colcha y sólo necesita un calcetín para terminarla.*

73. IMPORTANT SIGNS

Señores or *Hombres* or *Caballeros*	Men
Señoras or *Mujeres* or *Damas*	Women
Lavabo or *Lavatorio*	Lavatory
Cerrado	Closed
Abierto	Open
Prohibido fumar	No Smoking
Se prohibe la entrada	No Admittance
Llame	Knock
Toque el timbre	Ring
Privado	Private
Información dentro	Inquire Within
¡Pare!	Stop!
¡Siga!	Go!
¡Cuidado!	Look out!
¡Peligro!	Danger!
¡Despacio!	Go slow!
Desvío	Detour
Precaución	Caution
Conserve su derecha	Keep to the right
Puente	Bridge
Prohibido el estacionamiento	No Parking

Consigna	Check Room
(oficina de) Cambio	Money Exchanged
Oficina de Información	Information
Sala de espera	Waiting Room
No asomarse (a la ventanilla)	Don't lean out (of the window)
Furgón	Freight Car
Ferrocarril	Railroad
Expreso	Express
Local	Local
Parada	Stop (bus, streetcar, etc.)
Prohibido fijar anuncios	Post No Bills
En reparación	Under Repair
Entrada	Entrance
Salida	Exit
Habitaciones amuebladas	Furnished Rooms
Pisos	Apartments
Recién pintado	Wet Paint
Cruce	Crossroads
Carnicería	Butcher ("Butcher's Shop")
Panadería	Bakery
Lechería	Dairy
Sastrería	Tailor Shop
Zapatería	Shoe Store
Peluquería, Barbería	Barber Shop
Ultramarinos	Grocer
Farmacia (Droguería, Botica)	Pharmacy, Drugstore
Confitería (Pastelería)	Confectioner, Candy Store
Papelería	Stationery Store
Buzón	Letter Box
Taberna	Saloon, Bar, Tavern

Comisaría	Police Station
Vinos	Wines
Gasolina	Gas Station
Librería	Book Store
Ayuntamiento	City Hall
Refrescos y bocadillos	Refreshments
(Agua) Fría	Cold (water)
(Agua) Caliente	Hot (water)

QUIZ 38

1. *Entrada*	1. No Smoking
2. *Desvío*	2. Express
3. *No asomarse (a la ventanilla)*	3. No Parking
4. *Cerrado*	4. Open
5. *Abierto*	5. Exit
6. *Prohibido fumar*	6. Information
7. *Expreso*	7. Detour
8. *Prohibido el estacionamiento*	8. Entrance
9. *Salida*	9. Closed
10. *Oficina de información*	10. Don't lean out (of the window)

ANSWERS

1—8; 2—7; 3—10; 4—9; 5—4; 6—1; 7—2; 8—3; 9—5; 10—6.

FINAL QUIZ

When you get 100% on this Quiz you can consider that you have mastered the course.

1. *¿Me hace el favor de _____ (tell me) dónde está la estación?*
   a. permítame
   b. decirme
   c. tráigame

2. ¿_____ (can) *usted decirme dónde está la casa de correos?*
   a. *puede*
   b. *tiene*
   c. *cuesta*

3. ¿*Dónde* _____ (is) *un buen restaurant?*
   a. *hace*
   b. *hay*
   c. *hoy*

4. _____ (bring me) *un poco de pan.*
   a. *conocerla*
   b. *permítame*
   c. *tráigame*

5. _____ (I need) *jabón.*
   a. *necesito*
   b. *tiene*
   c. *permita*

6. _____ (I would like) *un poco más de carne.*
   a. *tráigame*
   b. *me hace falta*
   c. *quisiera*

7. *Le* _____ (I introduce) *a mi amiga.*
   a. *presento*
   b. *tengo*
   c. *venga.*

8. ¿*Dónde* _____ (is) *el libro?*
   a. *está*
   b. *es*
   c. *este*

9. *Tenga* _____ (the goodness) *de hablar más despacio.*
   a. *la bondad*
   b. *el favor*
   c. *el gusto*

10. ¿_____ (Do you understand) *el español?*
    a. *entiendo*
    b. *habla usted*
    c. *entiende usted*

11. _____ (Go) *allá.*
    a. *vaya usted*
    b. *habla usted*
    c. *está usted*

12. _____ (Come) *en seguida.*
    a. *venga*
    b. *voy*
    c. *vamos*

13. ¿*Cómo se* _____ (call) *usted?*
    a. *lava*
    b. *llama*
    c. *llamas*

14. ¿*Qué día de la* _____ (week) *es hoy?*
    a. *semana*
    b. *mes*
    c. *año*

15. ¿*Qué* _____ (time) *es?*
    a. *hora*
    b. *ahora*
    c. *tengo*

16. *No* _____ (I have) *cigarrillos.*
    a. *tiempo*
    b. *tengo*
    c. *tener*

17. ¿_____ (Do you want) *algo de fruta?*
    a. *podría usted*
    b. *tiene usted*
    c. *quiere usted*

18. _____ (Allow me) *que le presente a mi amigo.*
    a. *déme*
    b. *permítame*
    c. *tráigame*

19. _____ (I'd like) *escribir una carta.*
    a. *quiere*
    b. *quisiera*
    c. *permítame*

20. ¿*Cuánto* _____ (costs) *un telegrama para Valencia?*
    a. *cuesta*
    b. *costar*
    c. *cuenta*

21. *Queremos* _____ (breakfast) *para tres personas.*
    a. *desayuno*
    b. *comida*
    c. *almuerzo*

22. *Es la* _____ (1:45)
    a. *una y treinta*
    b. *una y cuarenticinco*
    c. *una y quince*

23. *Venga* _____ (tomorrow morning).
    a. *ayer por la mañana*
    b. *mañana por la mañana*
    c. *mañana a mediodía*

24. *¿En qué* _____ (can I) *servirle?*
    a. *pueda*
    b. *puede*
    c. *puedo*

25. *No* _____ (has) *importancia.*
    a. *tenga*
    b. *tiene*
    c. *tenido*

ANSWERS

1 b.; 2 a.; 3 b.; 4 c.; 5 a.; 6 c.; 7 a.; 8 a.; 9 a.; 10 c.;
11 a.; 12 a.; 13 b.; 14 a.; 15 a.; 16 b.; 17 c.; 18 b.;
19 b.; 20 a.; 21 a.; 22 b.; 23 b.; 24 c.; 25 b.

SUMMARY OF SPANISH GRAMMAR

1. THE ALPHABET

Letter	Name	Letter	Name	Letter	Name
a	a	j	jota	r	ere
b	be	k	ka	rr	erre
c	ç	l	ele	s	ese
ch	che	ll	elle	t	te
d	de	m	eme	u	u
e	e	n	ene	v	ve
f	efe	ñ	eñe	w	doble ve
g	ge	o	o	x	equis
h	hache	p	pe	y	i griega
i	i	q	cu	z	zeta

2. PRONUNCIATION

SIMPLE VOWELS

a	as in *ah* or *father*.
e	as in *day*.
i	as in *machine*.
o	as in *open*.
u	as in *rule*.

VOWEL COMBINATIONS

{ **ai** **ay**	*ai* in *aisle*.	**ie**	*ye* in *yes*.
		io	*yo* in *yoke*.
au	*ou* in *out*.		
		ua	*wah*.
{ **ei** **ey**	*áy-ee*.		
		ou	*wo* in *woe*.
eu	*áy-oo*.		
		iu	*you*.
{ **oi** **oy**	*oy* in *boy*.	{ **ui** **uy**	*óo-ee*.
ia	*ya* in *yard*.		

CONSONANTS

Notice the following points:

b, v have the same sound. After a pause and after *m* or *n*, both are like *b* in *boy*. When the sound occurs between vowels you bring the upper and lower lips together and blow between them, the way you do when blowing dust from something.[1]

c before *o, a,* and *u,* and before consonants, is like *c* in *cut.*

c before *e* and *i* is pronounced in Spain like *th* in *thin.* In Spanish America it is pronounced like *s* in *see.*

ch as in *church.*

d after a pause or *n* and *l,* like *d.* When it occurs between vowels, like *th* in *that.*

g before *a, o,* and *u,* and before consonants, after a pause, and after *n,* like *g* in *go.*

g before *e* and *i* is a strong rasping *h* (the sound you make when you clear your throat).

h is not pronounced.

j is like *g* before *e* and *i* (see above).

ll is pronounced in Spain like *lli* in *million;* in many countries of Latin America like *y* in *yes.*

ñ is like *ni* in *onion* or *ny* in *canyon.*

qu is like *k.*

r is pronounced by tapping the tip of the tongue against the gum ridge back of the upper teeth.

rr is trilled several times.

---

[1]Many Spanish speakers make the same difference between *b* and *v* that we do in English. They pronounce *b* whenever a *b* appears in the spelling and a *v* whenever a *v* appears in the spelling.

s	as in *see*.
x	before a consonant like *s;* between vowels like *x (ks)* in *extra*. Sometimes, however, it is like the *x (gs)* in *examine*.
y	when it begins a word or syllable, like *y* in *yes*.
y	when it serves as a vowel, like *i*.
z	is pronounced the same as the Spanich *c* before *e* and *i* (see above).

3. STRESS

1. Stress the last syllable if the word ends in a consonant other than *n* or *s*.

ciudad	city

2. Stress the next to the last syllable if the word ends in a vowel or *n* or *s*.

amigo	friend
hablan	they speak

3. Otherwise stress the syllable that has the accent (').

inglés	English
teléfono	telephone

4. PUNCTUATION

There are several differences between Spanish and English. Notice:

1. Exclamation and question marks precede as well as follow the sentence:

¿Adónde va usted?	Where are you going?
¡Hombre! ¿Adónde va Ud.?	Man! Where are you going?
¡Venga!	Come!
¡Qué hermoso día!	What a beautiful day!

2. The question mark is placed before the question part of the sentence:

Juan, ¿a dónde vas?	John, where are you going?
Usted conoce al Sr. Díaz, ¿no es verdad?	You know Mr. Díaz, don't you?

3. Dashes are often used where we use quotation marks:

Muchas gracias—dijo.	"Thanks a lot," he said.
Esta mañana—dijo—, fui a la ciudad.	"This morning," he said, "I went downtown."
—¿Cómo está usted?	"How are you?"
—Muy bien, gracias.	"Very well, thank you."

4. Capitals are not used as frequently as in English. They are only used at the beginning of sentences and with proper nouns. *Yo* "I," adjectives of nationality, the days of the week and the months are not capitalized:

Somos americanos.	We're Americans.
El no es francés sino inglés.	He's not French but English.
Vendré el martes o el miércoles.	I'll come Tuesday or Wednesday.
Hoy es el primero de febrero.	Today is the first of February.

5. Suspension points (. . .) are used more frequently than in English to indicate interruption, hesitation, etc.

5. SOME ORTHOGRAPHIC SIGNS

1. The tilde (˜) is used over the letter *n* to indicate the sound of *ni* in *onion* or *ny* in *canyon*.

2. The diaeresis (¨) is used over *u* in the combination *gu* when it is pronounced *gw*.

vergüenza	shame
paragüero	umbrella man; umbrella stand

6. THE DEFINITE ARTICLE

	SINGULAR	PLURAL
Masculine	*el*	*los*
Feminine	*la*	*las*

SINGULAR

el muchacho	the boy
la muchacha	the girl

PLURAL

los muchachos	the boys
las muchachas	the girls

1. *El* is used before a feminine noun beginning with stressed *a* (or *ha*):

el agua	the water
But—	
las aguas	the waters
el hacha	the axe
But—	
las hachas	the axes

2. The neuter article *lo* is used before parts of speech other than nouns when they are used as nouns:

lo malo	what is bad, the bad part of it
lo hecho	what is done
lo dicho	what is said
lo útil	the useful
lo difícil	the difficult
lo posible	the possible
lo necesario	the necessary

3. The definite article is used:

a. with abstract nouns:

La verdad vale más que las riquezas.	Truth is worth more than riches.

b. with nouns referring to a class:

los soldados	soldiers
los generales	generals

c. with names of languages (except immediately after *hablar* or *en*):

Escribo el español.	I write Spanish.
Habla bien el español.	He or she speaks Spanish well.

But—

Dígalo Ud. en inglés.	Say it in English.
Hablo español.	I speak Spanish.

d. in expressions of time:

la una	one o'clock
las dos	two o'clock
las diez	ten o'clock

e. for the days of the week:

Abren los domingos a las dos y media.	They open Sundays at 2:30.
el lunes próximo	next Monday

f. for the year, seasons, etc.

el año 1945	the year 1945
Vino el año pasado.	He came last year.
la primavera	spring
En el invierno hace frío.	It's cold in winter.

g. with certain geographical names:

El Brasil	Brazil
El Canadá	Canada
El Perú	Peru
El Uruguay	Uruguay
El Ecuador	Ecuador
El Japón	Japan

Note: The definite article is used with parts of the body and articles of clothing:

Me duele la cabeza.	My head hurts.
Quítese el abrigo.	Take your coat off.

7. THE INDEFINITE ARTICLE

	SINGULAR	PLURAL
Masculine	*un*	*unos*
Feminine	*una*	*unas*

SINGULAR

un hombre	a man
una mujer	a woman
unos hombres	men, some (a few) men

PLURAL

unas mujeres	women, some (a few) women

1. *Unos (unas)* is often used where we use "some" or "a few" in English:

unos días	a few days

2. The indefinite article is omitted:

a. before rank, profession, trade, nationality, etc.:

Soy capitán.	I'm a captain.
Soy médico.	I'm a doctor.

Soy abogado.	I'm a lawyer.
Es profesor.	He's a teacher.
Soy norteamericano.	I'm an American.
Ella es española.	She's Spanish.

b. before *ciento* (or *cien*) "hundred," *cierto* "certain," *mil* "thousand":

cien hombres	a hundred men
cierto hombre	a certain man
mil hombres	a thousand men

c. in various idiomatic expressions, such as:

Salió sin sombrero.	He left without a hat.

8. CONTRACTIONS

1. *de* + *el* = *del*	of (from) the
del hermano	from (of) the brother
2. *a* + *el* = *al*	to the
al padre	to the father

9. THE DAYS OF THE WEEK

The days of the week are masculine and are not capitalized. The article is usually necessary, except after *ser:*

el domingo	Sunday
el lunes	Monday
el martes	Tuesday
el miércoles	Wednesday
el jueves	Thursday
el viernes	Friday
el sábado	Saturday
El domingo es el primer día de la semana.	Sunday is the first day of the week.

Van a visitarlos el domingo.	They're going to pay them a visit on Sunday.
Mañana es sábado.	Tomorrow is Saturday.

Notice that "on Sunday," "on Monday," etc., are *el domingo, el lunes*, etc.

10. THE NAMES OF THE MONTHS

The names of the months are masculine and are not capitalized. They are usually used without the definite article:

enero	January
febrero	February
marzo	March
abril	April
mayo	May
junio	June
julio	July
agosto	August
septiembre	September
octubre	October
noviembre	November
diciembre	December

11. THE NAMES OF THE SEASONS

el invierno	winter
la primavera	spring
el verano	summer
el otoño	fall

The names of seasons are usually not capitalized. They are preceded by the definite article but after *de* and *en* the article may or may not be used:

Hace frío en (el) invierno.	It's cold in (the) winter.
Trabajo durante los meses de verano.	I work during the summer months.

12. MASCULINE AND FEMININE GENDER

Nouns referring to males are masculine; nouns referring to females are feminine:

el padre	the father	*la madre*	the mother
el hijo	the son	*la hija*	the daughter
el hombre	the man	*la mujer*	the woman
el toro	the bull	*la vaca*	the cow
el gato	the tomcat	*la gata*	the she-cat

The masculine plural of certain nouns stands for both genders:

Los padres	the parents, the father and mother
los reyes	the king and queen
mis hermanos	my brothers and sisters

Masculine nouns and adjectives usually end in -*o*; feminine nouns and adjectives in -*a*.

MASCULINE NOUNS

1. Nouns ending in -*o* are usually masculine:

el cuerpo	the body
el cielo	the sky
el dinero	the money

   Common Exceptions:

la mano	the hand
la radio	the radio

2. Nouns ending in *r, n,* and *l* are generally masculine:

el calor	the heat
el pan	the bread
el sol	the sun

3. Names of trees, days of the week, months, oceans, rivers, mountains, and other parts of speech used as nouns are generally masculine:

el álamo	the poplar
el martes	Tuesday
el Atlántico	The Atlantic Ocean
el Tajo	The Tagus River
los Andes	The Andes
el ser joven	being young, the fact of being young

FEMININE NOUNS

1. Nouns ending in -a (also -dad, -tad, -tud, -ción, -sión, -ez, -umbre, -ie) are usually feminine:

la cabeza	the head
la ciudad	the city
la cantidad	quantity
la libertad	liberty
la virtud	virtue
la condición	the condition
la costumbre	the custom
tensión	tension
madurez	maturity

Common Exceptions:

el día	the day
el mapa	the map
el drama	the drama
el clima	the climate
el problema	the problem
el poeta	the poet

2. Names of cities, towns and fruits are feminine:

Barcelona es muy bonita.	Barcelona is very nice.
la naranja	the orange
la manzana	the apple

Note: Certain nouns differ in meaning depending on whether they take *el* or *la*:

el orden	order (arrangement)
el capital	capital (money)
el cura	priest

But—

la orden	order (command)
la capital	capital (city)
la cura	curé

13. THE PLURAL

1. Nouns ending in an unstressed vowel add -*s*:

el libro the book *los libros* the books

2. Nouns ending in a consonant add -*es*:

el avión the airplane
los aviones the airplanes

3. Nouns ending in -*z* change the *z* to *c* and then add *es*:

la luz	the light	*las luces*	the lights
el lápiz	the pencil	*los lápices*	the pencils

4. Some nouns are unchanged in the plural:

los martes Tuesdays
los Martínez the Martínez family

14. THE POSSESSIVE

English -'s or -s' is translated by *de* "of":

el libro de Juan	John's book ("the book of John")
los libros de los niños	the boys' books ("the books of the boys")

15. ADJECTIVES

1. Singular and Plural

SINGULAR

un muchacho alto	a tall boy
una muchacha alta	a tall girl

PLURAL

dos muchachos altos	two tall boys
dos muchachas altas	two tall girls

Notice that the adjective comes after the noun and is masculine if the noun is masculine, plural if the noun is plural, etc.

2. Feminine Endings

a. If the ending is *o*, it becomes *-a*:

MASCULINE		FEMININE	
alto	tall	*alta*	tall
rico	rich	*rica*	rich
bajo	low	*baja*	low

b. In other cases there is no change:

MASCULINE	FEMININE	
grande	*grande*	big, large
azul	*azul*	blue
cortés	*cortés*	polite
útil	*útil*	useful
triste	*triste*	sad

Examples:

una cosa útil	a useful thing
una majer triste	a sad woman
una muchacha cortés	a polite girl

    c. Adjectives of nationality add -*a* or change *o* to *a*:

MASCULINE	FEMININE	
español	*española*	Spanish
francés	*francesa*	French
inglés	*inglesa*	English
Americano	*Americana*	American

    Examples:

una señora inglesa	an English woman
la lengua española	the Spanish language

    d. Adjectives ending in -*án*[1] and -*or* add -*a*:

MASCULINE	FEMININE	
holgazán	*holgazana*	lazy
burlón	*burlona*	jesting
preguntón	*preguntona*	inquisitive
encantador	*encantadora*	charming
fascinador	*fascinadora*	fascinating

3. The following adjectives drop the final -*o* when they come before a masculine singular noun:

uno	one
bueno	good
malo	bad
alguno	some one
ninguno	no one
primero	first
tercero	third

    Examples:

un buen amigo	a good friend
ningún hombre	no man
el mal tiempo	the bad weather
el primer día	the first day

---

[1] Notice that the accent is dropped in the feminine.

4. *Grande* becomes *gran* when it comes before a singular noun:

un gran amigo	a great friend
un gran poeta	a great poet
un gran hombre	a great (important) man

But—

un hombre grande	a large (tall) man

5. *Santo* becomes *San* when it comes before a noun (except those beginning in *To-* and *Do-*):

San Juan	Saint John
San Luis	Saint Louis

But—

Santo Tomás	Saint Thomas
Santo Domingo	Saint Dominic

6. *Ciento* becomes *cien* before a noun:

cien dólares	a hundred dollars

16. POSITION OF ADJECTIVES

1. Descriptive adjectives usually follow the noun:

un libro blanco	a white book
una casa blanca	a white house
mi sombrero nuevo	my new hat
dinero español	Spanish money
un hombre inteligente	an intelligent man
huevos frescos	fresh eggs

2. Exceptions are adjectives which describe an inherent quality:

la blanca nieve	the white snow

3. Articles, numerals, possessives and quantitatives usually precede the noun:

un buen muchacho	a good boy
muchas personas	many persons
poca gente	few people
cuatro huevos	four eggs

4. Some descriptive adjectives can come either before or after the noun:

una niña pequeña or *una pequeña niña*	a little girl
un día hermoso or *un hermoso día*	a nice (beautiful) day
una linda muchacha or *una muchacha linda*	a pretty girl

Other common adjectives used this way are *bueno* "good," *malo* "bad" and *bonito* "pretty."

5. A few adjectives have one meaning when they come before a noun and another when they follow:

un hombre pobre	a poor man
¡Pobre hombre!	Poor man!
un hombre grande	a large (tall) man
un gran hombre	a great (important) man
un libro nuevo	a new (recent) book
un nuevo hombre	a different man
cierto hombre	a certain man
una noticia cierta	a true piece of news

17. COMPARISON

1. Regular Comparison

fácil	easy

más fácil	easier
menos fácil	less easy
el más fácil	the easiest
el menos fácil	the least easy

2. Irregular Comparison

bueno	good	*mejor*	better, best
malo	bad	*peor*	worse, worst
mucho	much	*más*	more, most
poco	little	*menos*	less, least
grande	great	{ *mayor* { *más grande*	
pequeño	small	{ *menor* { *más pequeño*	

Más grande means "larger," "bigger"; *mayor* means "older":

Esta mesa es más grande que aquélla.	This table is larger than that one.
Pedro es mayor que Juan.	Peter is older than John.

Similarly, *más pequeño* means "smaller"; *menor* means "younger."

3. "More (less)...than..." = *más (menos) ...que...*

El español es más fácil que el inglés.	Spanish is easier than English.
Es más inteligente de lo que parece.	He's more intelligent than he looks.

4. "As...as..." = *tan...como...* or *tanto ...como...*

a. before an adjective or adverb:

Tan fácil como...	As easy as..
El habla español tan bien como yo.	He speaks Spanish as well as I do.

b. before a noun:

| *Tiene tanto dinero como Ud.* | He has as much money as you. |

5. "The more (less)... the more (less)..." = *cuanto más (menos)... tanto más (menos)...*

| *Cuanto más le trate tanto más le agradará.* | The more you get to know him (deal with him) the more you like him. |

6. "Most" = *-ísimo*

| *Es muy útil.* | It's very useful. |
| *Es utilísimo.* | It's most useful. |

The *-isimo* form (called the "absolute superlative") always stands by itself (that is, never modifies another word).

18. PRONOUNS

Pronouns have different forms depending on whether they are:
1. the subject of a verb
2. used after a preposition
3. the object of a verb
4. used as indirect objects
5. used with reflexive verbs

1. Pronouns as the subject of a verb:

SINGULAR

yo	I
tú	you
él	he
ella	she
ello	it
usted	you *(polite)*

PLURAL

nosotros	we *(masc.)*
nosotras	we *(fem.)*
vosotros	you *(masc.)*
vosotras	you *(fem.)*
ellos	they *(masc.)*
ellas	they *(fem.)*
ustedes	you *(polite)*

SINGULAR

(yo) hablo	I speak
(tú) hablas	you speak *(familiar)*
(él) habla	he speaks
(ella) habla	she speaks
(usted) habla	you speak *(polite)*

PLURAL

(nosotros) hablamos	we speak *(masc.)*
(nosotras) hablamos	we speak *(fem.)*
(vosotros) habláis	you speak *(masc.)*
(vosotras) habláis	you speak *(fem.)*
(ellos) hablan	they speak *(masc.)*
(ellas) hablan	they speak *(fem.)*
(ustedes) hablan	you speak *(polite)*

The personal pronouns *yo, tú*, etc., are not ordinarily used. "I speak" is just *hablo*, "we speak" *hablamos*, etc. They are used for emphasis or clearness (*usted habla* "you speak" and *él habla* "he speaks").

2. Pronouns used after prepositions:

para mí	for me
para tí	for you *(fam.)*
para él	for him
para ella	for her
para usted	for you *(polite)*

para nosotros	for us *(masc.)*
para nosotras	for us *(fem.)*
para vosotros	for you *(masc.)*
para vosotras	for you *(fem.)*
para ellos	for them *(masc.)*
para ellas	for them *(fem.)*
para ustedes	for you *(polite)*

Notice that the form of the pronoun used after a preposition is the same as the form of the pronoun used before a verb, except for *mí* "me" and *tí* "you" *(fam.)*.

There is a special form for "with me," "with you" and "with him": *conmigo* "with me," *contigo* "with you" and *consigo* "with him."

3. Pronouns as direct objects:

me	me
te	you *(fam.)*
le	him, you *(polite)*
la	her
lo	it

nos	us
os	you
los	them, you *(polite)*
las	them *(fem.)*

4. Pronouns as indirect objects:

me	to me
te	to you *(fam.)*
le	to him, her, you *(polite)*

nos	to us
os	to you
les	to them *(masc.* and *fem.)*
	to you *(masc.* and *fem.) (polite)*

Le as indirect object means "to him," "to her," "to you" (usted), and *les* means "to them," "to you" (ustedes). The preposition *a* and the prepositional forms *él, ella, usted* and *ellos, ellas, ustedes*, are often added for clearness.

SHORT FORM

$$le\ doy = \begin{cases} \text{I give to him} \\ \text{I give to her} \\ \text{I give to you} \end{cases}$$

$$les\ doy = \begin{cases} \text{I give to them } (masc.) \\ \text{I give to them } (fem.) \\ \text{I give to you} \end{cases}$$

FULL FORM

le doy a él	I give (to) him
le doy a ella	I give (to) her
le doy a usted	I give (to) you
les doy a ellos	I give (to) them
les doy a ellas	I give (to) them
les doy a ustedes	I give (to) you

This double construction is used even when the object is a noun:

Le escribí a María ayer.	I wrote to Mary yesterday.

5. Reflexive pronouns:

Reflexive pronouns are used when a person (or thing) does something to himself, herself (or itself): e.g. "I wash myself."

me	myself
te	yourself (*fam.*)
se	himself, herself, yourself (*polite*)
nos	ourselves
os	yourselves
se	themselves, yourselves (*polite*)

For examples, see pp. 70 and 71.

19. POSITION OF PRONOUNS

1. When there are both direct and indirect object pronouns in a sentence (*he gives it to me*) the Spanish order is the following:

ENGLISH	SPANISH
1 2	*2 1*
He gives it to me.	*Me lo da.*
1 2	*2 1*
They give it to us.	*Nos lo dan.*

That is, the indirect pronoun precedes the direct. If both begin with *l,* the indirect (*le, les*) becomes *se:*

Se lo diré (instead of *le lo diré*).	I will tell it to him (to her, to you, etc.)

2. When *se* is present it comes before the other conjunctive pronouns. It denotes:
   a. an impersonal action:

Se dice.	It is said.
Se la trató bien.	She was treated well.

   b. a personal object (may or may not be reflexive):

Se lo dice.	He says it to him (her) *or* he says it to himself *or* she says it to herself.

3. If *se* is not present, the first pronoun of the group has the meaning of an indirect object and the second that of a direct object:

Me lo da.	He gives it to me.

4. Object pronouns come before the verb:

Le veo.	I see him.
Se lo da.	He gives it to him.

They come after an infinitive or present participle:

Tenerlo.	To have it.
Dárselo.	To give it to him.
Quiero verle.	I want to see him.
Voy a verle.	I'm going to see him.
Teniéndolo.	Having it.
Diciéndolo.	Saying it.
Estoy mirándole.	I am looking at him.

Object pronouns follow affirmative commands:

Tómalo.	Take it.
Dígamelo Ud.	Tell it to me.

They come before negative commands (these are always in the subjunctive):

No me lo diga Ud.	Don't tell me.

5. *Te* and *os* precede all pronouns except *se:*

Te lo diré.	I will tell it to you.

But—

Se te dijo.	It was told to you.

6. *Le lo, la, les, los,* and *las* take the last place before the verb:

Yo se lo doy.	I give it to him.
El se lo dijo.	He told it to him.

20. CONJUNCTIONS

y	and
o	or
pero	but
mas	but
que	that
pues	since, as
si	if

por que	why
porque	because
ni . . . ni	neither . . . nor

NOTES

1. *y* "and"

Roberto y Juan son hermanos.	Robert and John are brothers.

e is used instead of *y* before a word beginning with *i-* or *hi-*:

María e Isabel son primas.	Mary and Elizabeth are cousins.
Madre e hija.	Mother and daughter.

2. *o* "or"

Cinco o seis pesos.	Five or six pesos.
Voy con mi hermano o con mi hermana.	I'm going with my brother or with my sister.

u is used instead of *o* before a word beginning with *o-* or *ho-*:

Siete u ocho horas.	Seven or eight hours.
Cinco u ocho meses.	Five or eight months.

3. *pero* "but"

Quiero venir pero no puedo.	I want to come but I can't.

4. *mas* "but" is more formal and literary:

Pensé que vendría mas no pudo.	I thought he would come but he wasn't able to.

5. *sino* "but" is used instead of *pero* after a negative statement:

No es francés sino inglés.	He is not French but English.
No viene hoy sino mañana.	He is not coming today but tomorrow.

21. QUESTION WORDS

1. *¿Qué?*   What?
¿Qué dice usted?   What are you saying?

2. *¿Por qué?*   Why?
¿Por qué dice usted eso?   Why do you say that?

3. *¿Cómo?*   How?
¿Cómo se dice en español esto?   How do you say this in Spanish?
¿Cómo se llama usted?   What's your name? ("How do you call yourself?")

4. *¿Cuánto?*   How much?
¿Cuánto dinero necesita usted?   How much money do you need?
¿Cuántos libros hay?   How many books are there?
¿Cuánto hay de Madrid a Barcelona?   How far is it from Madrid to Barcelona?

5. *¿Cuál?*   What? Which one?
¿Cuál es su nombre?   What's your name?
¿Cuál quiere usted?   Which one do you want?

6. *¿Quién?*   Who?
¿Quién vino con usted?   Who came with you?
¿Quién tiene eso?   Who has that?

7. *¿Dónde?*   Where?
¿Dónde está su amigo?   Where is your friend?

8. *¿Cuándo?*   When?
¿Cuándo se marcha Ud?   When are you going (leaving)?
¿Cuándo ocurrió eso?   When did that happen?

Notice that the question words are written with an accent.

22. ADVERBS

1. Spanish *-mente* corresponds to "*-ly*" in English. It is added to the feminine form of the adjective:

exclusivamente　　　　exclusively

When there are two adverbs, the ending *-mente* is added only to the last one:

clara y concisamente　　clearly and concisely

Adverbs are compared like adjectives.

POSITIVE	*alegremente*	cheerfully
COMPARATIVE		more cheerfully,
SUPERLATIVE	*más alegremente*	most cheerfully

2. Irregular Comparatives:

POSITIVE		COMPARATIVE	
bien	well	*mejor*	better, best
mal	badly	*peor*	worse, worst
mucho	much	*más*	more, most
poco	little	*menos*	less, least

3. Adverbs as prepositions or conjunctions. Many adverbs act as prepositions when *de* is added:

ADVERB:	*después*	afterwards
PREPOSITION:	*después de las cinco*	after five o'clock
ADVERB:	*además*	besides
PREPOSITION:	*además de*	besides

When *que* is added they act as conjunctions:

después de que venga　　after he comes

Other words which act similarly: *antes* "before"; *cerca* "near"; *delante* "before," "in front of"; *enfrente* "opposite."

4. Adverbs of time:

hoy	today
ayer	yesterday
mañana	tomorrow
temprano	early
tarde	late
a menudo	often
siempre	always
nunca	never
jamás	never
luego	afterwards
aprisa	quickly
despacio	slowly
antes que	before
después	afterwards

5. Adverbs of place:

aquí	here
acá	here (motion)
ahí	there
allí	there (farther away)
allá	there (motion)
adelante	forward, on
atrás	behind
dentro	inside
arriba	up, above
fuera	outside
abajo	down, below
cerca	near
lejos	far

6. Adverbs of quantity:

muy	very
mucho	much
poco	little
más	more
menos	less

además	besides
cuan	how much
cuanto	how much
tan	so much
tanto	so much
demasiado	too much
apenas	scarcely

7. Adverbs expressing affirmation:

sí	yes
verdaderamente	truly
cierto	certainly
ciertamente	certainly
claro	of course
desde luego	of course
por supuesto	of course

8. Adverbs expressing negation:

no	no, not
nunca	never
jamás	never
nunca jamás	never (more emphatic)
ya no	no more, not now
todavía no	not yet
tampoco	neither, either
no tal	no indeed
ni	nor
ni . . . ni	neither . . . not
ni siquiera	not even

9. Here and There:

Aquí "here" refers to something near the speaker:

Tengo aquí los libros.	I have the books here.

Ahí "there" refers to something near the person spoken to:

¿Qué tiene Ud. ahí?	What do you have there?
¿Está Ud. ahí?	Are you there?

Acá "here" expresses motion toward the speaker:

¡Venga Ud. acá!	Come here!

Allá "there" indicates motion away from the speaker:

¡Vaya Ud. allá!	Go there!
Va allá.	He's going there.

Allí "there" refers to something remote from both:

Vienen de allí.	They come from there.
Viví en Sud América por varios años. ¿Ha estado Ud. allí?	I've lived in South America for several years. Have you ever been there?

23. DIMINUTIVES AND AUGMENTATIVES

The endings *-ito* (*-cito, -ecito*), *-illo* (*-cillo, -ecillo*), *-uelo* (*-zuelo, -ezuelo*) imply smallness. In addition, *ito* often implies attractiveness or admiration, *-illo* and *-uelo* unattractiveness or depreciation. (They should be used with care.)

chico	boy	*chiquillo*	little boy
señora	lady, Mrs.	*señorita*	young lady, Miss
un poco	a little	*un poquito*	a little bit
pedazo	piece	*pedacito*	a little piece
gato	cat	*gatito*	kitten
papá	papa	*papaíto*	daddy
cuchara	tablespoon	*cucharita*	teaspoon
Venecia	Venice	*Venezuela*	Venezuela ("little Venice")
cigarro	cigar	*cigarrillo*	cigarette
autor	author	*autorcillo*	unimportant author

The ending *-ón (ona)* and *-ote* indicate largeness (often awkwardness and unattractiveness as well):

tonto	foolish, silly fool	*tontón*	big fool
silla	chair	*sillón*	big chair
cuchara	spoon	*cucharón*	a ladle
hombre	man	*hombrón*	he-man

24. DEMONSTRATIVES

1. Demonstrative Adjectives:

MASCULINE	FEMININE	
este	*esta*	this
ese	*esa*	that
aquel	*aquella*	that (farther removed)
estos	*estas*	these
esos	*esas*	those
aquellos	*aquellas*	those (farther removed)

a. Spanish demonstrative adjectives usually precede the nouns they modify and always agree in gender and number:

este muchacho	this boy
aquellos vecinos	those neighbors

b. *Ese* and *aquel* both mean "that." *Aquel* points out a thing removed in space or time from the speaker or from the person spoken to:

Esa señora es muy amable.	This lady is very kind.
Aquel señor que llegó el mes pasado.	That gentleman who arrived last month.

2. Demonstrative Pronouns:

MASCULINE	FEMININE	
éste	ésta	this (one)
ése	ésa	that (one)
aquél	aquélla	that (one)
éstos	éstas	these
ésos	ésas	those
aquéllos	aquéllas	those

NEUTER	
esto	this (one)
eso	that (one)
aquello	that (one)

The same difference exists between the pronouns *ése* and *aquél* as between the adjectives *ese* and *aquel:*

No quería éste sino aquél.	I didn't want this one but the one over there.

Este and *aquél* also mean "the latter" and "the former":

Acaban de llegar el embajador y su secretario.	The ambassador and his secretary just arrived.
Este es joven y aquél es viejo.	The former is old and the latter is young.

Notice that the Spanish order is the opposite of the English: *éste . . . aquél* ("the latter . . . the former").

The neuter demonstrative pronouns *esto, eso* and *aquello* refer to an idea previously stated and not to a specific thing:

Me dijo que aquello fué horrible.	He told me that that was horrible.

25. INDEFINITE ADJECTIVES AND PRONOUNS

todos	all
tal	such
ni uno	not one
otro	other
alguien	someone
nadie	nobody
algo	something, anything
ninguno	no one, none
alguno	someone
varios	several
nada	nothing
cualquiera	whatever, whoever
quienquiera	whoever

26. NEGATION

1. *No* "not" comes before the verb:

No veo.	I don't see.
El no habla	He isn't speaking.

2. There are two forms for "nothing," "never," "no one," etc.—one with and one without *no:*

No veo nada.	I see nothing.
No voy nunca.	I never go.
No viene nadie.	No one comes.
Or—	
Nada veo.	I see nothing
Nunca voy.	I never go.
Nadie viene.	No one comes.

27. WORD ORDER

1. The usual order is subject—verb—adverb—object:

Juan vió allí a sus amigos.	John saw his friends there.

2. The tendency in Spanish is to put the longer member of the sentence or the emphasized part last:

Me dió una carta.	He gave me a letter.
¿Compró la casa su señor padre?	Did your father buy the house?
Han caído veinte soldados.	Twenty soldiers were killed.

3. As in English, questions sometimes have the same order as statements but with the question intonation (that is, with a rise in pitch at the end):

¿Juan va a ir allí?	John is going to go there?

4. However, the more usual way of asking a question is to put the subject after the verb:

¿Va a ir allí Juan?	Is John going to go there?
¿Viene su amigo?	Is your friend coming?
¿Ha comido Ud.?	Have you eaten?
¿Habla usted español?	Do you speak Spanish?
¿Tiene usted dinero?	Do you have any money?
¿Por qué volvió Ud.?	Why did you return?
¿Ha recibido Juan mi carta?	Did John get my letter?

5. Adjectives come right after *ser*:

¿Es tarde?	Is it late?
¿Es bueno?	Is it good?
¿Es difícil la prueba?	Is the test difficult?
¿Es fácil el problema?	Is the problem easy?

28. THE TENSES OF THE VERB

Spanish verbs are divided into three classes ("conjugations") according to their infinitives:

Class I —*hablar*
Class II —*comer*
Class III—*vivir*

1. The Present:

I	II	III
-*o*	-*o*	-*o*
-*as*	-*es*	-*es*
-*a*	-*e*	-*e*
-*amos*	-*emos*	-*imos*
-*áis*	-*éis*	-*ís*
-*an*	-*en*	-*en*

hablar to speak	*comer* to eat	*vivir* to live
hablo	*como*	*vivo*
hablas	*comes*	*vives*
habla	*come*	*vive*
hablamos	*comemos*	*vivimos*
habláis	*coméis*	*vivís*
hablan	*comen*	*viven*

The following verbs insert *g* in the first person singular of the present indicative:

tener—tengo	I have
venir—vengo	I come
traer—traigo	I bring
poner—pongo	I put
hacer—hago	I do
decir—digo	I say
salir—salgo	I leave

The present can be translated in several ways:

Hablo español. {
I speak Spanish
I am speaking Spanish.
I do speak Spanish.
}

2. The Imperfect:

I	II AND III
-aba	*-ía*
-abas	*-ías*
-aba	*-ía*
-ábamos	*-íamos*
-abais	*-íais*
-aban	*-ían*

a. The imperfect is used:

1. to indicate continued or customary action in the past:

Cuando yo estaba en Madrid, siempre visitaba los teatros. — When I was in Madrid, I always used to visit the theaters.

Le encontraba todos los días. — I used to meet him every day.

2. to indicate what was happening when something else happened:

El escribía cuando ella entró. — He was writing when she entered.

b. Irregular Imperfects:

The following are the only Spanish verbs which are irregular in the imperfect:

ser—era, eras, era, éramos, erais, eran
ir—iba, ibas, iba, íbamos, ibais, iban
ver—veía, veías, veía, veíamos, veíais, veían

3. **The Future:**

The future of regular verbs is formed by adding to the infinitive the ending *-é, -ás, -á, -emos, -éis, -án:*

hablar to speak	*comer* to eat	*vivir* to live
hablaré	*comeré*	*viviré*
hablarás	*comerás*	*vivirás*
hablará	*comerá*	*vivirá*
hablaremos	*comeremos*	*viviremos*
hablaréis	*comeréis*	*viviréis*
hablarán	*comerán*	*vivirán*

The future generally expresses a future action:

Lo compraré.	I'll buy it.
Iré mañana.	I'll go tomorrow.

Sometimes it expresses probability or conjecture:

¿Qué hora será?	What time can it be? What time do you think it must be?
Será la una.	It must be almost one.
Estará comiendo ahora.	He's probably eating now.

4. **The Preterite:**

There are two sets of preterite endings:

1. One set is used with the stem of Conjugation I *(-ar):*

2. The other set is used with the stem of Conjugation II *(-er)* and Conjugation III *(-ir):*

-é	*-í*
-aste	*-iste*
-ó	*-ió*
-amos	*-imos*
-asteis	*-isteis*
-aron	*-ieron*

The preterite expresses an action that began in the past and ended in the past:

El lo dijo.	He said it.
Habló conmigo.	He spoke with me.
Fuí alli.	I went there.
El nos vió.	He saw us.
Escribí una carta.	I wrote a letter.
Llovió todo el día.	It rained all day.
El tren se paró.	The train stopped.
Pasó tres años allí.	He spent three years there.
Lo ví.	I saw him (it).

5. The Present Perfect:

The present perfect is formed by adding the past participle to the present tense of *haber*. It is used to indicate a past action which continues into the present or which ended only recently:

Ha venido con su amigo.	He has come with his friend.
Nos ha escrito.	He has written to us.

6. The Pluperfect:

The pluperfect is formed by adding the past participle to the imperfect of *haber*. It translates the English pluperfect:

Ya habían llegado.	They had already arrived.

7. The Future Perfect:

The future perfect is formed by adding the past participle to the future of *haber*. It translates the English future perfect:

Habrán llegado para entonces.	They will have arrived by then.

Sometimes it indicates probability:

Habrán llegado ayer.	They probably arrived yesterday.

8. The Preterite Perfect[1]:

The preterite perfect, which is rather rare, is formed by adding the past participle to the preterite of *haber*. It is used to indicate that something has occurred immediately before some other action in the past:

Apenas hubo oído eso, se marchó.	No sooner had he heard that than he left.

29. THE SUBJUNCTIVE

The indicative simply makes a statement; the subjunctive indicates a certain attitude towards the statement—uncertainty, desire, emotion, etc. The subjunctive is used in subordinate clauses when the statement is unreal, doubtful, indefinite, subject to some condition or is affected by will, emotion, etc.

1. Forms
    a. The subjunctive endings of the second and third conjugations are the same.
    b. The present subjunctive is formed by adding the subjunctive endings to the stem of the first person singular, present indicative; the imperfect and future subjunctive, by adding the endings of the stem of the third person plural, preterite.

The subjunctive endings are as follows:

Conjugation I

PRES. SUBJ.:	*-e, -es, -e, -emos, -éis, -en*
IMPERF. SUBJ.:	*-ara, -aras, -ara, -áramos, -arais, -aran*
	Or—
	-ase, -ases, -ase, -ásemos, -aseis, -asen

[1]Also called "past anterior."

| FUTURE SUBJ.: | *(-are, -ares, -are, -áremos, -areis, -aren)*[1] |

Conjugations II and III

| PRES. SUBJ.: | *-a, -as, -a, -amos, -áis, -an* |
| IMPERF. SUBJ.: | *-iera, -ieras, -iera, -iéramos, -ierais, -ieran* |

Or

-iese, -ieses, -iese, -iésemos, -ieseis, -iesen

| FUTURE SUBJ.: | *(-iere, -ieres, -iere, -iéremos, -iereis, -ieren)* |

EXAMPLES

	I	II	III
INFINITIVE:	*hablar*	*comer*	*vivir*
PRES. SUBJ.:	*hable*	*coma*	*viva*
IMPERF. SUBJ.:	*hablara*	*comiera*	*viviera*
	hablase	*comiese*	*viviese*
FUTURE SUBJ.:	*(hablare*	*comiere*	*viviere)*
	(hablare	*comiere*	*viviere)*

2. Uses

    a. The subjunctive is used with verbs of desire, request, suggestion, permission, approval and disapproval, judgment, opinion, uncertainty, emotion, surprise, fear, denial, etc.:

Quisiera verle.	I'd like to see him.
¡Ojalá que lo haga!	I wish he would do it!
¡Ojalá lo supiera!	I wish I knew it!
Temo que se lo diga él.	I'm afraid he may tell it to him.
No creo que él le haya visto.	I don't believe he's seen him.
Niega que le haya visto.	He denies that he's seen him.
Me sorprende mucho que él no lo haya hecho.	I'm greatly surprised that he hasn't done it.

[1] Forms in parentheses are rare.

Espero que no venga.	I hope he doesn't come.
Me alegro de que Ud. esté aquí.	I'm glad you're here!
Temo que esté enfermo.	I'm afraid he's sick.
Temo que no llegue a tiempo.	I'm afraid he won't (mayn't) come in time.
Duda que lo hagamos.	He doubts that we'll do it.
Dudo que sea verdad.	I doubt that it's true.
Dudo que sea posible.	I doubt whether it's possible.
No creo que lo sepa.	I don't think he knows it.
Se lo digo para que lo sepa.	I'm telling you so you may know it.

b. The subjunctive is used in commands:

    1. Affirmative or negative commands in the polite form:

¡Abra usted la ventana!	Open the window!
¡No hablen ustedes ahora!	Don't talk now!

    2. Negative commands in the familiar form:

No me digas (tú).	Don't tell me!
No habléis ahora.	Don't talk now!

    3. Suggestions in which the speaker is included:

Leamos.	Let's read!
Entremos.	Let's go in!

    4. Indirect commands (that is, commands in the third person):

Que vaya él.	Let him go.
¡Viva España!	Long live Spain!
¡Que vengan!	Let them come!
¡Que entren!	Let them come in!
¡Que no venga!	Let him not come!

c. The subjunctive is used in conditional sentences which are contrary to fact:

Si estaba allí, yo no le ví.	If he was there, I didn't see him. *(Indicative)*
No iremos si llueve.	If it rains, we won't go. *(Indicative)*

But—

Si fuese él, lo haría.	If I were him (he), I'd do it.
Si fuera mío esto, lo vendería.	If this were mine, I'd sell it.
Si tuviera el dinero, lo compraría.	If I had the money, I'd buy it.
Aunque hubiese tenido dinero no hubiera ido.	Even if I had had the money I wouldn't have gone.
Si lo hubiera sabido, no habría venido.	If I had known it, I wouldn't have come.
Si hubiese estado aquí, habríamos ido.	If he had been here, we would have gone.
Aunque lo hubiese intentado no hubiera podido hacerlo.	Even if I would have tried, I wouldn't have been able to do it.

d. The subjunctive is used after impersonal verbs which do not express certainty:

Es menester que vengan.	It's necessary for them to come.
Es preciso que estén aquí.	It's necessary for them to be here.
Es necesario que Ud. venga.	It's necessary that you come.
Es posible que lo tenga.	It's possible that he has it.
Era lástima que no vinieran.	It was a pity that they didn't come.

e. The subjunctive is used after various conjunctive adverbs:

1. Certain conjunctive adverbs are always followed by the subjunctive because they never introduce statements of accomplished fact:

antes (de) que	before
a condición de	on condition that
aunque	even if
a (fin de) que	in order that
a menos que	unless
como si	as if
con tal (de) que	provided that, providing
dado que	granted that, given . . .
no obstante que	notwithstanding that
supuesto que	supposing that

2. Other conjunctive adverbs may or may not introduce a statement of accomplished fact. When they do, they take the indicative; otherwise the subjunctive:

a menos que	unless
a pesar de que	in spite of, notwithstanding
antes que	before
así que	as soon as
aunque	although, even though
con tal que	provided (that)
cuando	when
de manera que	so that
de modo que	so that
después (de) que	after
en cuanto	as soon as
hasta que	until
luego que	as soon as
mientras que	as long as, while
para que	in order that, so that
siempre que	provided that, whenever
Aunque él no lo quiera, se lo daré.	I'll give it to him even though he may not want it.

Lo compraré aunque me cueste mucho.	I'll buy it even if it costs me a lot.
Se lo digo para que lo sepa.	I'm telling you so that you may know it.
Aunque llueva mañana.	Although it may rain tomorrow.
Se fué sin que lo supiésemos.	He went away without our knowing it.
Iré con Ud. con tal que tenga tiempo.	I'll go with you provided I have time.
En caso que llegue.	In case he arrives.
Compare:	
Iremos aunque llueve.	We'll go even though it's raining.
Iremos aunque llueva.	We'll go even if it rains (even if it should rain).

   f. The subjunctive is used when an indefinite antecedent is limited by an adjective (relative) clause:

No hay ningún hombre que entienda esto.	There is no man who understands this.
Busco a alguien que hable español.	I'm looking for someone who speaks Spanish.
No conozco a nadie que pueda hacerlo.	I don't know anyone who can do it (could do it).

   g. The subjunctive is used after compounds of *-quiera* "-ever": *quienquiera* "whoever," *dondequiera* "wherever," *cualquier* "whatever," "whichever":

Quienquiera que sea.	Whoever he (it) may be.
El quiere hacer cualquier cosa que ella haga.	He wants to do whatever she does.
El quiere ir dondequiera que ella vaya.	He wants to go wherever she goes.

30. THE CONDITIONAL

1. The present conditional of all verbs is formed by adding to the infinitive the endings of the imperfect indicative of haber: *ía, ías, íamos, íais, ían*. It translates the English "would" or "should":

I	II	III
hablar to speak	*comer* to eat	*vivir* to live
hablaría	*comería*	*viviría*
hablarías	*comerías*	*vivirías*
hablaría	*comería*	*viviría*
hablaríamos	*comeríamos*	*viviríamos*
hablaríais	*comeríais*	*viviríais*
hablarían	*comerían*	*vivirían*

Sometimes it expresses probability or conjecture:

| *Serían las dos cuando él llegó.* | It was probably about two o'clock when he arrived. |
| *¿Qué hora sería?* | What time could it have been? |

2. The perfect conditional is formed by adding the past participle to the conditional of *haber*. It translates the English "would have" or "should have":

| *Habría hablado.* | I would have spoken. |
| *Habría ido* | I would have gone. |

3. If a sentence contains a clause beginning with *si* "if," the tense of the verb is determined by the tense of the verb in the main clause.

If the main clause has a verb in the:	The "if" clause has a verb in the:
Present	Present
Future	Present
Imperfect	Imperfect
Preterite	Preterite
Conditional	Past Subjunctive (-ra or -se)

Si está aquí, trabaja.	If he is here, he is working.
Si estaba aquí, trabajaba.	If he was here, he was working.
Si está aquí mañana, trabajará.	If he's here tomorrow, he'll be working.
Si estuviera aquí, trabajería.	If he were here, he'd be working.

A main verb indicating a condition contrary to fact may be in the -ra form of the subjunctive.

Si estuviera aquí, trabajara.	If he were here, he'd be working.

31. COMMANDS AND REQUESTS (THE IMPERATIVE)

There are two types of commands, one with *tú (vosotros)* and one with *usted (ustedes)*.

1. Familiar Commands *(Tú)*

   Familiar commands are used with people to whom you would say *tú*. The singular is the same as the third person singular of the present indicative:

¡Habla (tú)!	Speak!
¡Come (tú)!	Eat!
¡Sube (tú)!	Go up!

   The plural is always formed by removing the -*r* of the infinitive and adding -*d:*

I

hablar to speak

SINGULAR:	¡Habla (tú)!	Speak!
PLURAL:	¡Hablad (vosotros, -as)!	Speak!

II

apprender to learn

SINGULAR:	¡Aprende (tú)!	Learn!
PLURAL:	¡Aprended (vosotros, -as)!	Learn!

III

escribir to write

PLURAL:	¡Escribe (tú)!	Write!
SINGULAR:	¡Escribid (vosotros, -as)!	Write!

Common exceptions in the singular (the plural is always regular):

		IMPERATIVE	
INFINITIVE		SINGULAR	PLURAL
ser	to be	sé	sed
decir	to say	dí	decid
ir	to go	ve	id
hacer	to do	haz	haced
poner	to put	pon	poned
tener	to hold	ten	tened
venir	to come	ven	venid

Familiar commands in the negative are in the present subjunctive:

SINGULAR

¡No hables!	Don't speak!
¡No me hables!	Don't talk to me!
¡No comas!	Don't eat!

PLURAL

¡No habléis!	Don't speak!
¡No comáis!	Don't eat!

Other Examples:

¡Háblame!	Speak to me!
¡Háblales!	Speak to them!
¡No les hables!	Don't speak to them!
¡Hablad!	Speak!
¡No habléis!	Don't speak!
¡Dame!	Give me!
¡No me des!	Don't give me!
¡Dímelo!	Tell it to me!
¡No me lo digas (tú)!	Don't tell it to me!
¡No me digas (tú) eso!	Don't tell me that!
¡Decídnoslo!	Tell it to us!
¡No nos lo digáis!	Don't tell it to us!
¡No estudiéis demasiado!	Don't study too much!

Notice that the object pronouns follow the affirmative imperative and precede the negative imperative.

2. Polite Commands *(Usted)*
   Polite commands are used with people to whom you would say *usted* and are in the subjunctive. To make the subjunctive you change the ending of the third person present indicative to *a* if it is *e*, or to *e* if it is *a*.

INDICATIVE		SUBJUNCTIVE	
Habla.	He speaks.	*Hable Ud.*	Speak!
Come.	He eats.	*Come Ud.*	Eat!

The plural is formed by adding *n* to the singular:

¡Hablen Uds.!	Speak!
¡Coman Uds.!	Eat!
¡Desciendan Uds.!	Go down!

Other Examples:

¡Cómalo (Ud.)!	Eat it!
¡Venga (Ud.) a verme!	Come to see me!
¡Tómelo!	Take it!
¡Dígamelo!	Tell it to me!
¡Escríbame (Ud.) una carta!	Write me a letter!
¡Escríbamelo!	Write it to me!
¡Abra (Ud.) la ventana!	Open the window!

NEGATIVE

¡No hable Ud.!	Don't speak!
¡No lo coma Ud.!	Don't eat it!
¡No me lo diga Ud.!	Don't tell me!
¡No me escriba Ud.!	Don't write to me!
¡No hablen Uds. demasiado!	Don't talk too much!

The pronoun objects follow the affirmative imperative and are attached to it:

¡Léelo (tú)!	Read it!
¡Habladle!	Speak to him!
¡Véndamelo!	Sell it to me!
¡Dígamelo!	Tell it to me!

3. Indirect Commands

Indirect commands are in the subjunctive and are usually preceded by *que:*

¡Que entren!	Let them come in!
¡Qué él lo haga!	Let him do it!
¡Que lo haga Juan!	Let John do it!
¡Que le habla María!	Let Mary talk to him!
¡Que venga!	Let him come!
¡Que vaya él!	Let him go!
¡Que no venga!	Let him not come!
¡Viva España!	Long live Spain!
¡Dios guarde a nuestro país!	God keep our country!

4. "Let's" is expressed by the subjunctive:

¡Hablemos un rato!	Let's talk a while!
¡No hablemos!	Let's not talk!
¡Vayamos!	Let's go!
¡Esperemos!	Let's wait!

5. Imperative of Reflexive Verbs
   The final *-d* of the plural is dropped when *-os* is added; that is, *"sentados"* becomes *sentaos:*

FAMILIAR FORM
SINGULAR

¡Siéntate!	Sit down!
¡Despiértate!	Wake up!
¡No te sientes!	Don't sit down!

PLURAL

¡Sentaos!	Sit down!
¡Despertaos!	Wake up!
(despertad + os)	
¡No os sentéis!	Don't sit down!

POLITE FORM
SINGULAR

¡Siéntese Ud.!	Sit down!
¡No se siente Ud.!	Don't sit down!

PLURAL

¡Siéntense Uds.!	Sit down *(pl.)*!
¡No se sienten!	Don't sit down!
¡Sentémonos!	Let's sit down!
(sentemos + nos)	

32. THE PARTICIPLE

1. The present participle (also called the "gerund") of Conjugation I is formed by dropping the *-ar* of the infinitive and adding *-ando;* the present participle of Conjugations II and III is

made by dropping the *-er (-ir)* and adding *-iendo:*

	I		II
hablar	to speak	*comer*	to eat
hablando	speaking	*comiendo*	eating

	III	
	vivir	to live
	viviendo	living

Pronoun objects are attached to the present participle (in such cases the verb has a written accent):

comprándolos	buying them
vendiéndomelo	selling it to me
dándoselo	giving it to him

The present participle is often used absolutely, describing some action or state of being of the subject of the sentence:

Durmiendo, no me oyeron.	Since they were sleeping, they didn't hear me. They didn't hear me because they were sleeping.
Estando cansandos, dormían.	Being tired, they were sleeping. They were taking a nap because they were tired.

2. The past participle is formed by adding *-ado* to the stem of *-ar* verbs (that is, the infinitive minus *-ar*) and *-ido* to the stem of *-er* and *-ir* verbs:

	I		II
hablar	to speak	*comer*	to eat
hablado	spoken	*comido*	eaten

III

vivir	to live	
vivido	lived	

3. Irregular Participles
   The following are some of the commonest verbs
   with irregular present and past participles:

INFINITIVE		IRREGULAR PAST PARTICIPLE	IRREGULAR PRESENT PARTICIPLE
abrir	to open	*abierto*	
caer	to fall	*caído*	*cayendo*
creer	to believe	*creído*	*creyendo*
cubrir	to cover	*cubierto*	
decir	to say	*dicho*	*diciendo*
despedirse	to take leave of		*despidiéndose*
dormir	to sleep		*durmiendo*
escribir	to write	*escrito*	
hacer	to do, make	*hecho*	
ir	to go		*yendo*
leer	to read	*leído*	*leyendo*

INFINITIVE		IRREGULAR PAST PARTICIPLE	IRREGULAR PRESENT PARTICIPLE
morir	to die	*muerto*	*muriendo*
oir	to hear		*oyendo*
pedir	to ask for		*pidiendo*
poder	to be able to		*pudiendo*
poner	to put	*puesto*	
seguir	to follow		*siguiendo*
sentir	to feel		*sintiendo*
traer	to bring	*traído*	*trayendo*
venir	to come		*viniendo*
ver	to see	*visto*	
volver	to return	*vuelto*	

33. PROGRESSIVE TENSES

The Spanish progressive tenses are made up of the forms of *estar* plus the present participle. As in English, they denote a continuing action (that is, they describe the action as going on):

Estoy trabajando aquí.	I'm working here.
Estábamos leyendo un periódico.	We were reading a newspaper.
Estoy divirtiéndome.	I'm having a good time.
Está hablando.	He's speaking.
Estaba esperándome.	He was waiting for me.

34. PASSIVE VOICE

The passive voice is made up of the forms of *ser* plus the past participle:

La carta fué escrita por ella.	The letter was written by her.

The passive is used as in English. Very often, however, Spanish uses the reflexive where English uses the passive (see p. 70):

Aquí se habla inglés.	English is spoken here.

35. TO BE

There are two words in Spanish for "to be": *ser* and *estar*. In general *ser* indicates a permanent state (I'm an American); *estar* a temporary one (I'm tired).

SER	ESTAR	
yo soy	*yo estoy*	I am
tú eres	*tú estás*	you are
usted es	*usted está*	you are

él es	él está	he is
ella es	ella está	she is
ello es	ello está	it is
nosotros somos	nosotros estamos	we are
nosotras somos	nosotras estamos	we are
vosotros sois	vosotros estáis	you are
vosotras sois	vosotras estáis	you are
ustedes son	ustedes están	you are
ellos son	ellos están	they are
ellas son	ellas están	they are

SER

1. indicates a permanent condition or state:

Mi hermano es alto.	My brother is tall.

2. is used with a predicate noun, in which case it links two equal things:

El es médico.	He is a doctor.
Es escritor.	He's a writer.
Es español.	He's a Spaniard.

3. is used with an adjective to indicate an inherent quality.

El libro es rojo.	The book is red.
Ella es joven.	She is young.
El hielo es frío.	Ice is cold.
Es inteligente.	He's intelligent.
Es encantadora.	She's charming.

4. is used with pronouns:

Soy yo.	It's I.

5. indicates origin, source or material:

¿De dónde es Ud.?	Where are you from?
Soy de España.	I'm from Spain.
Es de madera.	It's made of wood.
Es de plata.	It's silver.

6. indicates possession:

¿De quién es esto?	Whose is this?
Los libros son del señor Díaz.	The books belong to Mr. Diaz.

7. is used in telling time:

Es la una.	It's one o'clock.
Son las dos.	It's two o'clock.
Son las nueve y diez.	It's ten past nine.

8. is used to indicate cost:

Son a quince centavos la docena.	They are fifteen cents a dozen.
Son a nueve dólares cada uno.	They are nine dollars each.

9. is used in impersonal constructions:

Es tarde.	It's late.
Es temprano.	It's early.
Es necesario.	It's necessary.
Es lástima.	It's a pity.
¿No es verdad?	Isn't it?

ESTAR

1. expresses position or location:

Está allí.	He's over there.
Está en México.	He's in Mexico.
Nueva York está en los Estados Unidos.	New York is in the United States.
Los Andes están en Sud América.	The Andes are in South America.
El Canal está en Panamá.	The Canal is in Panama.
¿Dónde está el libro?	Where's the book?
Está sobre la mesa.	It's on the table.

2. indicates a temporary quality or characteristic:

Ella está contenta.	She's pleased.
Estoy cansado.	I'm tired.
Estoy listo.	I'm ready.
El café está frío.	The coffee's cold.
Está claro.	It's clear.
La ventana está abierta (cerrada).	The window's open (shut).

3. is used to form the present progressive tense:

Están hablando.	They are talking.
Están caminando.	They are walking. They keep (on) walking.

4. is used in the expression "How are you?" etc.:

¿Cómo está Ud.?	How are you?
¿Cómo están ellos?	How are they?

Some adjectives may be used with either *ser* or *estar* with a difference in meaning.

El es malo.	He is bad.
El está malo.	He is sick.
Es pálida.	She has a pale complexion.
Está pálida.	She is pale (at this moment).

	With *ser*	With *estar*
bueno	good	well, in good health
listo	clever	ready, prepared
cansado	tiresome	tired

THE FORMS OF THE REGULAR VERBS

A. CONJUGATIONS I, II, III

INDICATIVE AND CONDITIONAL

INFINITIVE	PRES. & PAST PARTICIPLES	PRESENT INDICATIVE	IMPERFECT	PRETERITE	FUTURE	CONDITIONAL	PRESENT PERFECT	PLUPERFECT	PRETERITE PERFECT
I. -*ar* ending *hablar* to speak	hablando hablado	hablo hablas habla hablamos habláis hablan	hablaba hablabas hablaba hablábamos hablabais hablaban	hablé hablaste habló hablamos hablasteis hablaron	hablaré hablarás hablará hablaremos hablaréis hablarán	hablaría hablarías hablaría hablaríamos hablaríais hablarían	he has ha + hablado hemos habéis han	había habías había + hablado habíamos habíais habían	hube hubiste hubo + hablado hubimos hubisteis hubieron
II. -*er* ending *comer* to eat	comiendo comido	como comes come comemos coméis comen	comía comías comía comíamos comíais comían	comí comiste comió comimos comisteis comieron	comeré comerás comerá comeremos comeréis comerán	comería comerías comería comeríamos comeríais comerían	he has ha + comido hemos habéis han	había habías había + comido habíamos habíais habían	hube hubiste hubo + comido hubimos hubisteis hubieron
III. -*ir* ending *vivir* to live	viviendo vivido	vivo vives vive vivimos vivís viven	vivía vivías vivía vivíamos vivíais vivían	viví viviste vivió vivimos vivisteis vivieron	viviré vivirás vivirá viviremos viviréis vivirán	viviría vivirías viviría viviríamos viviríais viviríanhan	he has ha + vivido hemos habéis han	había habías había + vivido habíamos habíais habían	hube hubiste hubo + vivido hubimos hubisteis hubieron

Group 1 (hablar)

FUTURE PERFECT	CONDITIONAL PERFECT	SUBJUNCTIVE						IMPERATIVE
		PRESENT	IMPERFECT (-r-)	IMPERFECT (-s-)	PRESENT PERFECT	PLUPERFECT (-r-)	PLUPERFECT (-s-)	
habré	habría	hable	hablara	hablase	haya	hubiera	hubiese	¡Habla (tú)!
habrás	habrías	hables	hablaras	hablases	hayas	hubieras	hubieses	¡Hable (Ud.)!
habrá + hablado	habría + hablado	hable	hablara	hablase	haya + hablado	hubiera + hablado	hubiese + hablado	¡Hablemos (nosotros)!
habremos	habríamos	hablemos	habláramos	hablásemos	hayamos	hubiéramos	hubiésemos	¡Hablad (vosotros)!
habréis	habríais	habléis	hablarais	hablaseis	hayáis	hubierais	hubieseis	¡Hablen (Uds.)!
habrán	habrían	hablen	hablaran	hablasen	hayan	hubieran	hubiesen	

Group 2 (comer)

FUTURE PERFECT	CONDITIONAL PERFECT	SUBJUNCTIVE						IMPERATIVE
		PRESENT	IMPERFECT (-r-)	IMPERFECT (-s-)	PRESENT PERFECT	PLUPERFECT (-r-)	PLUPERFECT (-s-)	
habré	habría	coma	comiera	comiese	haya	hubiera	hubiese	¡Come (tú)!
habrás	habrías	comas	comieras	comieses	hayas	hubieras	hubieses	¡Coma (Ud.)!
habrá + comido	habría + comido	coma	comiera	comiese	haya + comido	hubiera + comido	hubiese + comido	¡Comamos (nosotros)!
habremos	habríamos	comamos	comiéramos	comiésemos	hayamos	hubiéramos	hubiésemos	¡Comed (vosotros)!
habréis	habríais	comáis	comierais	comieseis	hayáis	hubierais	hubieseis	¡Coman (Uds.)!
habrán	habrían	coman	comieran	comiesen	hayan	hubieran	hubiesen	

Group 3 (vivir)

FUTURE PERFECT	CONDITIONAL PERFECT	SUBJUNCTIVE						IMPERATIVE
		PRESENT	IMPERFECT (-r-)	IMPERFECT (-s-)	PRESENT PERFECT	PLUPERFECT (-r-)	PLUPERFECT (-s-)	
habré	habría	viva	viviera	viviese	haya	hubiera	hubiese	¡Vive (tú)!
habrás	habrías	vivas	vivieras	vivieses	hayas	hubieras	hubieses	¡Viva (Ud.)!
habrá + vivido	habría + vivido	viva	viviera	viviese	haya + vivido	hubiera + vivido	hubiese + vivido	¡Vivamos (nosotros)!
habremos	habríamos	vivamos	viviéramos	viviésemos	hayamos	hubiéramos	hubiésemos	¡Vivid (vosotros)!
habréis	habríais	viváis	vivierais	vivieseis	hayáis	hubierais	hubieseis	¡Vivan (Uds.)!
habrán	habrían	vivan	vivieran	viviesen	hayan	hubieran	hubiesen	

B. RADICAL CHANGING VERBS
1. Group I: *-ar* and *-er* verbs only

a) Change the *o* to *ue* when stress falls on root (ex: *contar, volver*).
b) Change the *e* to *ie* when stress falls on root (ex: *pensar, perder*).

INFINITIVE*	PRESENT INDICATIVE	PRESENT SUBJUNCTIVE	IMPERATIVE	SIMILARLY CONJUGATED VERBS		
contar(ue) to count	cuento cuentas cuenta contamos contáis cuentan	cuente cuentes cuente contemos contéis cuenten	cuenta contad	acordar acordarse acostarse almorzar apostar aprobar	avergonzar avergonzarse colgar costar encontrar jugar (*u* to *ue*)	probar recordar recordarse sonar soñar volar
volver(ue) to return	vuelvo vuelves vuelve volvemos volvéis vuelven	vuelva vuelvas vuelva volvamos volváis vuelvan	vuelve volved	devolver doler dolerse llover morder mover	oler soler	

268

	Present Indicative	Present Subjunctive	Imperative			
pensar(ie) to think	pienso piensas piensa pensamos pensáis piensan	piense pienses piense pensemos penséis piensen	piensa pensad	acertar apretar calentar cerrar confesar despertar	empezar encerrar gobernar plegar quebrar sentarse	temblar tentar
perder(ie) to lose	pierdo pierdes pierde perdemos perdéis pierden	pierda pierdas pierda perdamos perdáis pierdan	pierde perded	ascender atender defender descender encender entender	extender tender	

*In all the other tenses, these verbs are conjugated like all other regular verbs.

B. RADICAL CHANGING VERBS

2. Group II: -ir verbs only

a) Change o to ue when stress falls on root (ex: dormir).
b) Change o to u when stress falls on ending (ex: dormir—present subj. only).
c) Change e to ie when stress falls on root (ex: sentir).
d) Change e to i when stress falls on ending (ex: sentir—present subj. only).

INFINITIVE*	PRESENT INDICATIVE	PRESENT SUBJUNCTIVE	IMPERATIVE	SIMILARLY CONJUGATED VERBS
dormir to sleep	duermo duermes duerme dormimos dormís duermen	duerma duermas duerma durmamos durmáis duerman	duerme dormid	morir (past parti.: muerto)
sentir to feel	siento sientes siente sentimos sentís sienten	sienta sientas sienta sintamos sintáis sientan	siente sentid	advertir herir arrepentirse mentir consentir preferir convertir presentir diferir referir divertir sugerir

*In all the other tenses, these verbs are conjugated like all other regular verbs.

270

3. Group III: *-ir* verbs only

Change *e* to *i* when stress falls on root: (ex: *pedir*)

INFINITIVE†	PRESENT INDICATIVE	PRESENT SUBJUNCTIVE	PRETERITE INDICATIVE	IMPERFECT SUBJUNCTIVE	IMPERATIVE	SIMILARLY CONJUGATED VERBS	
pedir to ask	pido pides pide pedimos pedís piden	pida pidas pida pidamos pidáis pidan	pedí pediste pidió pedimos pedisteis pidieron	pidiera (se) pidieras (ses) pidiera (se) pidiéramos (semos) pidierais (seis) pidieran (sen)	pide pedid	competir conseguir corregir despedir despedirse elegir	expedir reír repetir seguir servir vestir

†In all the other tenses, these verbs are conjugated like all other regular verbs.

271

C. REGULAR VERBS
WITH SPELLING CHANGES

1. VERBS ENDING IN -car

Example: buscar to look for

Verbs ending in *-car; c* changes to *qu* when followed by *e.* This occurs in:

1. the first person singular of the preterite
2. all persons of the present subjunctive

PRETERITE INDICATIVE	PRESENT SUBJUNCTIVE
busqué	*busque*
buscaste	*busques*
buscó	*busque*
buscamos	*busquemos*
buscasteis	*busquéis*
buscaron	*busquen*

Verbs conjugated like *buscar:*

acercar	to place near	*sacrificar*	to sacrifice
educar	to educate	*secar*	to dry
explicar	to explain	*significar*	to signify, mean
fabricar	to manufacture	*tocar*	to touch, play
indicar	to indicate		(music)
pecar	to sin	*verificar*	to verify
sacar	to take out		

2. VERBS ENDING IN -gar

Example: *pagar* to pay

Verbs ending in *-gar: g* changes to *gu* when followed by *e.* This occurs in:

1. the first person singular of the preterite indicative

2. all persons of the present subjunctive

PRETERITE INDICATIVE	PRESENT SUBJUNCTIVE
pagué	*pague*
pagaste	*pagues*
pagó	*pague*
pagamos	*paguemos*
pagasteis	*paguéis*
pagaron	*paguen*

Verbs conjugated like *pagar:*

ahogar	to drown	*investigar*	to investigate
apagar	to extinguish	*juzgar*	to judge
arriesgar	to risk	*llegar*	to arrive
cargar	to load	*obligar*	to compel
castigar	to punish	*otorgar*	to grant
congregar	to congregate	*pegar*	to hit
entregar	to deliver	*tragar*	to swallow

3. VERBS ENDING IN -*guar*

Example. *averiguar* to ascertain, investigate

Verbs ending in -*guar: gu* changes to *gü* when followed by *e*. This occurs in:

1. the first person singular of the preterite indicative
2. all persons of the present subjunctive

PRETERITE INDICATIVE	PRESENT SUBJUNCTIVE
averigüé	*averigüe*
averiguaste	*averigües*
averiguó	*averigüe*
averiguamos	*averigüemos*
averiguasteis	*averigüéis*
averiguaron	*averigüen*

Verbs conjugated like *averiguar:*

aguar	to water, dilute
atestiguar	to attest

4. VERBS ENDING IN -*zar*

Example: *gozar* to enjoy

Verbs ending in -*zar*: *z* changes to *c* when followed by *e*. This occurs in:

1. the first person singular of the preterite indicative
2. all persons of the present subjunctive

PRETERITE INDICATIVE	PRESENT SUBJUNCTIVE
gocé	*goce*
gozaste	*goces*
gozó	*goce*
gozamos	*gocemos*
gozasteis	*gocéis*
gozaron	*gocen*

Verbs conjugated like *gozar*:

abrazar	to embrace	*organizar*	to organize
alcanzar	to reach	*rechazar*	to reach
cruzar	to cross	*rezar*	to pray
enlazar	to join	*utilizar*	to utilize

5. VERBS ENDING IN -*ger*

Example: *coger* to catch

Verbs ending in -*ger*: *g* changes to *j* when followed by *o* or *a*. This occurs in:

1. the first person singular of the present indicative
2. all persons of the present subjunctive

PRESENT INDICATIVE	PRESENT SUBJUNCTIVE
cojo	*coja*
coges	*cojas*
coge	*coja*
cogemos	*cojamos*
cogéis	*cojáis*
cogen	*cojan*

Verbs conjugated like *coger:*

acoger	to welcome	*proteger*	to protect
escoger	to choose, select	*recoger*	to gather

6. VERBS ENDING IN -*gir*

Example: *dirigir* to direct

Verbs ending in -*gir:* *g* changes to *j* when followed by *o* or *a*. This occurs in:

1. the first person singular of the present indicative
2. all persons of the present subjunctive

dirijo	*dirija*
diriges	*dirijas*
dirige	*dirija*
dirigimos	*dirijamos*
dirigís	*dirijáis*
dirigen	*dirijan*

Verbs conjugated like *dirigir:*

afligir	to afflict	*rugir*	to roar
erigir	to erect	*surgir*	to come forth
exigir	to demand		

7. VERBS ENDING IN -*guir*

Example: *distinguir* to distinguish

Verbs ending in -*guir:* *gu* changes to *g* when followed by *o* or *a*. This occurs in:

1. the first person singular of the present indicative
2. all persons of the present subjunctive

PRESENT INDICATIVE	PRESENT SUBJUNCTIVE
distingo	*distinga*
distingues	*distingas*
distingue	*distinga*

distinguimos	*distingamos*
distinguís	*distingáis*
distinguen	*distingan*

Verbs conjugated like *distinguir:*

conseguir	to get, obtain	*perseguir*	to persecute
extinguir	to extinguish	*seguir*	to follow

8. VERBS ENDING IN *-cer, -cir*

(Preceded by a vowel)

Examples: *conocer* to know *lucir* to shine

Some verbs ending in *-cer, -cir,* preceded by a vowel, change *c* to *zc* before *o* or *a*. This occurs in:

1. the first person singular of the present indicative
2. all persons of the present subjunctive

conozco	*conozca*	*luzco*	*luzca*
conoces	*conozcas*	*luces*	*luzcas*
conoce	*conozca*	*luce*	*luzca*
conocemos	*conozcamos*	*lucimos*	*luzcamos*
conocéis	*conozcáis*	*lucís*	*luzcáis*
conocen	*conozcan*	*lucen*	*luzcan*

Verbs conjugated like *conocer:*

aborrecer	to hate	*desaparecer*	to disappear
acaecer	to happen	*desobedecer*	to disobey
acontecer	to happen	*desvanecer*	to vanish
agradecer	to be grateful	*embellecer*	to embellish
amanecer	to dawn	*envejecer*	to grow old
anochecer	to grow dark	*fallecer*	to die
aparecer	to appear	*favorecer*	to favor
carecer	to lack	*merecer*	to merit
compadecer	to pity	*nacer*	to be born
complacer	to please	*obedecer*	to obey
conducir	to conduict	*ofrecer*	to offer
crecer	to grow	*oscurecer*	to grow dark

padecer	to suffer	*placer*	to please
parecer	to seem	*reconocer*	to recognize
permanecer	to last	*traducir*	to translate
pertenecer	to belong to		

9. VERBS ENDING IN -*cer*
(Preceded by a Consonant)

Example: *vencer* to conquer

Verbs ending in -*cer*, preceded by a consonant: *c* changes to *z* when followed by *e* or *a*. This occurs in:

1. the first person singular of the present indicative
2. all persons of the present subjunctive

PRESENT INDICATIVE	PRESENT SUBJUNCTIVE
venzo	*venza*
vences	*venzas*
vence	*venza*
vencemos	*venzamos*
vencéis	*venzáis*
vencen	*venzan*

Verbs conjugated like *vencer:*

convencer to convince *ejecer* to exercise

10. VERBS ENDING IN -*uir*
(But not -*guir* and -*quir*)

Example: *construir* to build

Verbs ending in -*uir*, except those ending in -*guir* or *quir*, add *y* to the stem of the verb before *a, e, o*. This occurs in:

1. all persons of the present indicative (except the first and second familiar persons plural)
2. all persons of the present and imperfect subjunctive
3. the imperative singular *(tú)*
4. third singular and plural of the preterite

PRESENT INDICATIVE	PRESENT SUBJUNCTIVE
construyo	*construya*
construyes	*construyas*
construye	*construya*
construimos	*construyamos*
construís	*construyáis*
construyen	*construyan*

(*i* between two other vowels changes to *y*)

PRETERITE INDICATIVE	IMPERFECT SUBJUNCTIVE
construí	*construyera (se)*
construiste	*construyeras (ses)*
construyó	*construyera (se)*
construimos	*construyéramos (semos)*
construisteis	*construyerais (seis)*
construyeron	*construyeran (sen)*

IMPERATIVE

construye
construid

Verbs conjugated like *construir:*

atribuir	to attribute	*huir*	to flee
constituir	to constitute	*influir*	to influence
contribuir	to contribute	*instruir*	to instruct
destituir	to deprive	*reconstruir*	to rebuild
destruir	to destroy	*restituir*	to restore
distribuir	to distribute	*substituir*	to substitute
excluir	to exclude		

11. VERBS LIKE *Creer*

Creer to believe

In verbs whose stem ends in *e*, the *i* of the regular endings beginning with *-ie, ió*, becomes *y*. This occurs in:

1. the present participle *creyendo*.

2. the third person singular and plural of the preterite indicative

3. both forms of the imperfect subjunctive

PRETERITE INDICATIVE	IMPERFECT SUBJUNCTIVE
creí	*creyera (se)*
creiste	*creyeras (ses)*
creyó	*creyera (se)*
creimos	*creyéramos (semos)*
creísteis	*creyerais (seis)*
creyeron	*creyeran (sen)*

Verbs conjugated like creer:

caer	to fall (irregular)	*leer*	to read
construir	to build	*poseer*	to possess

12. VERBS LIKE *Reír*

Reír to laugh

In verbs whose stem ends in *i*, the *i* of the regular endings, -*ie*, -*ió*, is dropped to avoid two *i*'s. This occurs in:

1. the present participle *riendo*

2. the third person singular and plural of the preterite indicative

3. all persons of both forms of the imperfect subjunctive

PRETERITE INDICATIVE	IMPERFECT SUBJUNCTIVE
reí	*riera (se)*
reiste	*rieras (ses)*
rió	*riera (se)*

reímos	riéramos (semos)
reísteis	rierais (seis)
rieron	rieran

Verbs conjugated like *reír; sonreír* to smile.

13. VERBS ENDING IN *-ller, -llir, -ñer, -ñir*

Example: *tañer* to toll

Present Participle: *tañendo*

PRETERITE INDICATIVE	IMPERFECT SUBJUNCTIVE
tañí	tañera (se)
tañiste	tañeras (ses)
tañó	tañera (se)
tañimos	tañéramos (semos)
tañisteis	tañerais (seis)
tañeron	tañeran (sen)

In verbs whose stem ends in *ll* or *ñ*, the *i* of the regular endings beginning with *-ie, -ió* is dropped. This occurs in:

1. the present participle
2. the third person singular and plural of the preterite indicative
3. all persons of both forms of the imperfect subjunctive

Verbs conjugated like *tañer:*

bullir	to boil	*gruñir*	to growl

14. VERBS ENDING IN *-iar, -uar*

Examples: *enviar* to send   *continuar* to contine

PRES. IND.	PRES. SUBJ.	PRES. IND.	PRES. SUBJ.
envío	envíe	continúo	continúe
envías	envíes	continúas	continúes
envía	envíe	continúa	continúe

enviamos	enviemos	continuamos	continuemos
enviáis	enviéis	continuáis	continuéis
envían	envíen	continúan	continúen

IMPERATIVE

| envía | continúa |
| enviad | continuad |

Some verbs ending in *-iar* or *-uar* take a written accent over the *i* or the *u* of the stem. There is no definite rule.

1. in all persons of the present indicative (except the first plural and second plural familiar).
2. in all persons of the present subjunctive (except the first plural and the second plural familiar).
3. in the singular of the imperative *(tú)*.

Verbs conjugated like *enviar:*

confiar	to trust	desconfiar	to distrust
criar	to bring up	fiar	to give credit
desafiar	to challenge	guiar	to guide

Verbs conjugated like *continuar:*

| actuar | to act | evaluar | to evaluate |
| efectuar | to carry out | perpetuar | to perpetuate |

THE FORMS OF THE IRREGULAR VERBS*

INFINITIVE, PRESENT AND PAST PARTICIPLES	PRESENT INDICATIVE	PRESENT SUBJUNCTIVE	IMPERFECT	PRETERITE	FUTURE	CONDITIONAL	IMPERATIVE
andar "to walk" *andando* *andado*	ando andas anda andamos andáis andan	ande andes ande andemos andéis anden	andaba andabas andaba andábamos andabais andaban	anduve anduviste anduvo anduvimos anduvisteis anduvieron	andaré andarás andará andaremos andaréis andarán	andaría andarías andaría andaríamos andaríais andarían	anda andad
caber "to fit," "to be contained in" *cabiendo* *cabido*	quepo cabes abe cabemos cabéis caben	quepa quepas quepa quepamos quepáis quepan	cabía cabías cabía cabíamos cabíais cabían	cupe cupiste cupo cupimos cupisteis cupieron	cabré cabrás cabrá cabremos cabréis cabrán	cabría cabrías cabría cabríamos cabríais cabrían	cabe cabed
caer "to fall" *cayendo* *caído*	caigo caes cae caemos caéis caen	caiga caigas caiga caigamos caigáis caigan	caía caías caía caíamos caíais caían	caí caiste cayó caimos caisteis cayeron	caeré caerás caerá caeremos caeréis caerán	caería caerías caería caeríamos caeríais caerían	cae caed
conducir "to lead," "to drive" *conduciendo* *conducido*	conduzco conduces conduce conducimos conducís conducen	conduzca conduzcas conduzca conduzcamos conduzcáis conduzcan	conducía conducías conducía conducíamos conducíais conducían	conduje condujiste condujo condujimos condujisteis condujeron	conduciré conducirás conducirá conduciremos conduciréis conducirán	conduciría conducirías conduciría conduciríamos conduciríais conducirían	conduce conducid

282

dar "to give" dando dado	doy das da damos dais dan	dé des dé demos déis den	daba dabas daba dábamos dabais daban	di diste dió dimos disteis dieron	daré darás dará daremos daréis darán	daría darías daría daríamos daríais darían	da dad
decir "to say," "to tell" diciendo dicho	digo dices dice decimos decís dicen	diga digas diga digamos digáis digan	decía decías decía decíamos decíais decían	dije dijiste dijo dijimos dijisteis dijeron	diré dirás dirá diremos diréis dirán	diría dirías diría diríamos diríais dirían	di decid
estar "to be" estando estado	estoy estás está estamos estáis están	esté estés esté estemos estéis estén	estaba estabas estaba estábamos estabais estaban	estuve estuviste estuvo estuvimos estuvisteis estuvieron	estaré estarás estará estaremos estaréis estarán	estaría estarías estaría estaríamos estaríais estarían	está estad
haber "to have" (auxiliary) habiendo habido	he has ha hemos habéis han	haya hayas haya hayamos hayáis hayan	había habías había habíamos habíais habían	hube hubiste hubo hubimos hubisteis hubieron	habré habrás habrá habremos habréis habrán	habría habrías habría habríamos habríais habrían	

*To form compound tenses, use the appropriate form of *haber* together with the past participle of the irregular verb.

THE FORMS OF THE IRREGULAR VERBS*

INFINITIVE, PRESENT AND PAST PARTICIPLES	PRESENT INDICATIVE	PRESENT SUBJUNCTIVE	IMPERFECT	PRETERITE	FUTURE	CONDITIONAL	IMPERATIVE
hacer "to do," "to make" *haciendo* *hecho*	hago haces hace hacemos hacéis hacen	haga hagas haga hagamos hagáis hagan	hacía hacías hacía hacíamos hacíais hacían	hice hiciste hizo hicimos hicisteis hicieron	haré harás hará haremos haréis harán	haría harías haría haríamos haríais harían	haz haced
ir "to go" *yendo* *ido*	voy vas va vamos vais van	vaya vayas vaya vayamos vayáis vayan	iba ibas iba íbamos ibais iban	fui fuiste fué fuimos fuisteis fueron	iré irás irá iremos iréis irán	iría irías iría iríamos iríais irían	ve id
oír "to hear" *oyendo* *oído*	oigo oyes oye oímos oís oyen	oiga oigas oiga oigamos oigáis oigan	oía oías oía oíamos oíais oían	oí oíste oyó oímos oísteis oyeron	oiré oirás oirá oiremos oiréis oirán	oiría oirías oiría oiríamos oiríais oirían	oye oíd
poder "to be able," "can" *pudiendo* *podido*	puedo puedes puede podemos podéis pueden	pueda puedas pueda podamos podáis puedan	podía podías podía podíamos podíais podían	pude pudiste pudo pudimos pudisteis pudieron	podré podrás podrá podremos podréis podrán	podría podrías podría podríamos podríais podrían	puede poded

Infinitive	Present Indicative	Present Subjunctive	Imperfect	Preterite	Future	Conditional	Imperative
poner "to put," "to place" *poniendo* *puesto*	pongo pones pone ponemos ponéis ponen	ponga pongas ponga pongamos pongáis pongan	ponía ponías ponía poníamos poníais ponían	puse pusiste puso pusimos pusisteis pusieron	pondré pondrás pondrá pondremos pondréis pondrán	pondría pondrías pondría pondríamos pondríais pondrían	pon poned
querer "to want," "to love" *queriendo* *querido*	quiero quieres quiere queremos queréis quieren	quiera quieras quiera queramos queráis quieran	quería querías quería queríamos queríais querían	quise quisiste quiso quisimos quisisteis quisieron	querré querrás querrá querremos querréis querrán	querría querrías querría querríamos querríais querrían	quiere quered
reír "to laugh" *riendo* *reído*	río ríes ríe reímos reís ríen	ría rías ría riamos riáis rían	reía reías reía reíamos reíais reían	reí reíste rió reímos reísteis rieron	reiré reirás reirá reiremos reiréis reirán	reiría reirías reiría reiríamos reiríais reirían	ríe reíd
saber "to know" *sabiendo* *sabido*	sé sabes sabe sabemos sabéis saben	sepa sepas sepa sepamos sepáis sepan	sabía sabías sabía sabíamos sabíais sabían	supe supiste supo supimos supisteis supieron	sabré sabrás sabrá sabremos sabréis sabrán	sabría sabrías sabría sabríamos sabríais sabrían	sabe sabed

THE FORMS OF THE IRREGULAR VERBS*

INFINITIVE, PRESENT AND PAST PARTICIPLES	PRESENT INDICATIVE	PRESENT SUBJUNCTIVE	IMPERFECT	PRETERITE	FUTURE	CONDITIONAL	IMPERATIVE
salir "to go out," "to leave" *saliendo* *salido*	salgo sales sale salimos salís salen	salga salgas salga salgamos salgáis salgan	salía salías salía salíamos salíais salían	salí saliste salió salimos salisteis salieron	saldré saldrás saldrá saldremos saldréis saldrán	saldría saldrías saldría saldríamos saldríais saldrían	sal salid
ser "to be" *siendo* *sido*	soy eres es somos sois son	sea seas sea seamos seáis sean	era eras era éramos erais eran	same as preterite of *ir.*	seré serás será seremos seréis serán	sería serías sería seríamos seríais serían	sé sed
tener "to have" *teniendo* *tenido*	tengo tienes tiene tenemos tenéis tienen	tenga tengas tenga tengamos tengáis tengan	tenía tenías tenía teníamos teníais tenían	tuve tuviste tuvo tuvimos tuvisteis tuvieron	tendré tendrás tendrá tendremos tendréis tendrán	tendría tendrías tendría tendríamos tendríais tendrían	ten tened

286

Infinitive	Present	Pres. Subj.	Imperfect	Preterite	Future	Conditional	Imperative
traer "to bring" *trayendo* *traído*	traigo traes trae traemos traéis traen	traiga traigas traiga traigamos traigáis traigan	traía traías traía traíamos traíais traían	traje trajiste trajo trajimos trajisteis trajeron	traeré traerás traerá traeremos traeréis traerán	traería traerías traería traeríamos traeríais traerían	trae traed
valer "to be worth" *valiendo* *valido*	valgo vales vale valemos valéis valen	valga valgas valga valgamos valgáis valgan	valía valías valía valíamos valíais valían	valí valiste valió valimos valisteis valieron	valdré valdrás valdrá valdremos valdréis valdrán	valdría valdrías valdría valdríamos valdríais valdrían	val valed
venir "to come" *viniendo* *venido*	vengo vienes viene venimos venís vienen	venga vengas venga vengamos vengáis vengan	venía venías venía veníamos veníais venían	vine viniste vino vinimos vinisteis vinieron	vendré vendrás vendrá vendremos vendréis vendrán	vendría vendrías vendría vendríamos vendríais vendrían	ven venid
ver "to see" *viendo* *visto*	veo ves ve vemos veis ver	vea veas vea veamos veáis vean	veía veías veía veíamos veíais veían	vi viste vió vimos visteis vieron	veré verás verá veremos veréis verán	vería verías vería veríamos veríais verían	ve ved

LETTER WRITING

1. FORMAL INVITATIONS
ACCEPTANCES

INVITATIONS

marzo de 1985

Jorge Fernández y Sra.—Tienen el gusto de partici-
par a Ud. y familia el próximo enlace matrimonial de
su hija Carmen, con el Sr. Juan García y los invitan a
la Ceremonia que se verificará en la Iglesia de Nuestra Señora de la Merced, el día 6 de los corrientes, a
las 6 de la tarde. A continuación tendrá lugar una
recepción en la casa de los padres de la novia en honor
de los contrayentes.

March 1985

Mr. and Mrs. George Fernandez take pleasure in
announcing the wedding of their daughter Carmen to
Mr. Juan García, and invite you to the ceremony that
will take place at the Church of Nuestra Señora de la
Merced, on the 6th of this month at 6 p.m. There will
be a reception for the newlyweds afterwards at the
residence of the bride's parents.

Los señores de Suárez ofrecen sus respetos a los
señores García y les ruegan que les honren viniendo a
comer con ellos el lunes próximo, a las ocho.

Mr. and Mrs. de Suárez present their respects to
Mr. and Mrs. García and would be honored to have
their company at dinner next Monday at 8 o'clock.

Los señores de Suárez y Navarro saludan afectuosamente a los señores Del Vayo y les ruegan que les honren asistiendo a la recepción que darán en honor de su hija María, el domingo 19 de marzo, a las nueve de la noche.

Mr. and Mrs. de Suárez y Navarro ("greet Mr. and Mrs. Del Vayo cordially and") request the honor of their presence at the party given in honor of their daughter María, on Sunday evening, March 19, at nine o'clock.

ANSWERS

Los señores Del Vayo les agradecen infinito la invitación que se han dignado hacerles y tendrán el honor de asistir a la recepción del domingo 19 de marzo.

Thank you for your kind invitation. We shall be honored to attend the reception on March 19th.

Los señores García tendrán el honor de acudir al convite de los señores de Suárez y entretanto les saludan cordialmente.

Mr. and Mrs. García will be honored to have dinner with Mr. and Mrs. de Suárez. With kindest regards.

Los señores García ruegan a los señores de Suárez se sirvan recibir las gracias por su amable invitación y la expresión de su sentimiento al no poder aceptarla por hallarse comprometidos con anterioridad.

Mr. and Mrs. García thank Mr. and Mrs. de Suárez for their kind invitation and regret that they are unable to come owing to a previous engagement.

2. THANK-YOU NOTE

marzo 5 de 1985

Querida Anita,

La presente es con el fin de saludarte y darte las gracias por el precioso florero que me has enviado de regalo. Lo he colocado encima del piano y no te imaginas el lindo efecto que hace.

Espero verte pasado mañana en la fiesta que da Carmen, la cual parece que va a ser muy animada.

Deseo que estés bien en compañía de los tuyos. Nosotros sin novedad. Te saluda cariñosamente, tu amiga.

Vicenta

March 5, 1985

Dear Anita,

This is just to say hello and also to let you know that I received the beautiful vase you sent me as a gift. I've put it on the piano and you can't imagine the beautiful effect.

I hope to see you at Carmen's party tomorrow. I think it's going to be a very lively affair.

I hope your family is all well. Everyone here is fine.

Vicenta

3. BUSINESS LETTERS

Araujo & Co., Inc.
125 Paseo de Gracia
Barcelona—España

Abril 2 de 1985

González e hijos
Madrid—España

Muy señores nuestros:

Nos es grato presentarles al portador de la presente, Sr. Carlos de la Fuente, nuestro viajante, quien se propone visitar las principales poblaciones de esa región. No necesitamos decirles que cualquier atención que le dispensen la consideraremos como un favor personal. Anticipándoles las gracias, nos es grato reiterarnos de Uds. como siempre,

Sus Attos. y SS.SS.

Araujo & Co., Inc.

_____

Presidente.

Araujo & Co., Inc.
125 Paseo de Gracia
Barcelona—Spain

April 2, 1985

Gonzalez & Sons
Madrid
Spain

Gentlemen:

We have the pleasure of introducing to you the bearer of this letter, Mr. Carlos de la Fuente, one of our salesmen, who is visiting the principal cities of

your region. Needless to say, we shall greatly appreciate any courtesy you extend to him. ("It is needless to
say to you that we shall consider any courtesy you
extend him as a personal favor.") Thanking you in
advance, we remain

Very truly yours,
Araujo & Co., Inc.

_____

President

Panamá
marzo 3 de 1985

Sr. Julián Pérez
Buenos Aires, Apt. 22
Argentina

Muy Señor mío:

Sírvase encontrar adjunto un cheque de $5 por un
año de subscripción a la revista de su digna dirección.

Atentamente,

María Pérez de Perera
Apartado 98
Panamá, Dep. de Panamá

P.O. Box 98
Panama, Republic of Panama

March 3rd, 1985

Mr. Julián Pérez
Buenos Aires
P.O. Box 22
Argentina

Dear Sir:

Enclosed please find a check for $5.00 for a year's
subscription to your magazine.

Very truly yours,
Mrs. María Perera

4. INFORMAL LETTERS

Mi querido Pepe:

Me ha sido sumamente grato recibir tu última carta.
Ante todo déjame darte el gran notición. Pues he
decidido por fin hacer un viaje a Madrid, donde
pienso pasar todo el mes de mayo.

Vicenta se viene conmigo. A ella le encanta la idea
de conoceros. Me la traigo para que conozca a Madrid y al mismo tiempo para que le sirva de compañía
a tu mujer. De esta manera nuestras mujeres tendrán
una infinidad de chismes que contarse y así nos
dejarán una que otra tarde libre para que tú y yo
podamos estar a nuestras anchas. Por lo tanto, procura desligarte del mayor número posible de compro-
misos para entonces.

Los negocios marchan bien por ahora y confío que
continuará la buena racha. El otro día estuve con
Antonio y me preguntó por ti.

Procura mandar a reservarnos una habitación en el Nacional, que te lo agradeceré mucho.

Escríbeme pronto. Dale mis recuerdos a Elena y tú recibe un abrazo de tu amigo,

Juan

Dear Pepe,

I was very happy to get your last letter. First of all, let me give you the big news. I have finally decided to make a trip to Madrid, where I expect to spend all of May.

Vicenta is coming with me. She is extremely happy to be able to meet the two of you at last. I'm bringing her along so that she can see Madrid and also so that she can keep your wife company. In this way our wives will have a lot of gossip to share with one another and leave us a free afternoon in which we can be at our ease. Try therefore to be as free as you can then.

Business is good now and I hope will keep up that way ("that the good wind will continue"). I saw Anthony the other day and he asked me about you.

I'd appreciate your trying to reserve a room for us in the "National."

Write soon. Give my regards to Helen.

Yours,
John

5. FORMS OF SALUTATIONS AND COMPLIMENTARY CLOSINGS

1. Salutations:

FORMAL

Señor:	Sir:
Señora:	Madam:
Señorita:	Miss:

Muy señor mío:	Dear Sir;
Muy señores míos:	Gentlemen:
Estimado señor:	Dear Sir:
De mi consideración:	Dear Sir:
Muy distinguido señor:	Dear Sir:
Muy señor nuestro:	Dear Sir:
Muy señores nuestros:	Gentlemen:
Señor profesor:	My dear Professor:
Excelentísimo señor:	Dear Sir: ("Your Excellency:")
Estimado amigo:	Dear Friend:
Querido amigo:	Dear Friend:

INFORMAL

Don Antonio (Aguilera);	My dear Mr. Aguilera:
Doña María (de Suárez):	My dear Mrs. Suárez:
Señorita Vicenta (Suárez):	My dear Miss Suárez:
Antonio:	Anthony:
Querida Vicenta:	Dear Vicenta:
Mi querida Vicenta:	My dear Vicenta:
Amada mía:	My beloved:
Querida mía:	My dear,; My beloved:

2. Complimentary Closings:

FORMAL

The following are equivalent to our "Very sincerely yours":

Su Atto. y S.S. (Su atento y seguro servidor)

Sus Attos. y Ss. Ss. (Sus atentos y seguros servidores)

S.S.S. (Su seguro servidor)
Ss. Ss. Ss. (Sus seguros servidores)
Q.B.S.P. (Que besa sus pies) (*(to a lady)*)
Q.E.S.M. (Que estrecha sus manos)

INFORMAL

Cariñosamente.	Affectionately yours,
Atentamente.	Sincerely yours,
Sinceramente.	Sincerely yours,
Afectuosamente.	Affectionately yours,
Quien mucho le aprecia.	Affectionately,
De quien te estima.	Affectionately,
De su amigo que le quiere.	Affectionately,
De tu querida hija.	Your loving daughter,
Besos y abrazos. **De todo corazón.** **De quien la dora.**	With love,

3. Form of the Letter:

FORMAL

Estimado Señor:
or Muy señor mío:
  (Dear Sir:)

_____

_____

_____

Atto. y S.S.[1]
(Yours truly,)

___

[1] *Atto. y S.S.* stands for *atento y seguro servidor.*

Querido Juan:
(Dear John,)

_____

_____

_____

Cariñosamente,
(Affectionately,)

_or_

Afectuosamente,
(Affectionately,)

4. Common formulas:

Beginning a letter–

1. Me es grato acusar recibo de su atenta del 8 del corriente. Tengo el agrado de... This is to acknowledge receipt of your letter of the 8th of this month. I am glad to...

2. Obra en mi poder su apreciable carta de fecha 10 de marzo... I have received your letter of March 10th.

3. En contestación a su atenta carta de ayer... In answer to your letter of yesterday...

4. De conformidad con su grata del... In accordance with your letter of...

5. Con referencia a su anuncio en "La Nación" de hoy... In reference to your ad in today's issue of "The Nation,"...

6. Por la presente me dirijo a Ud. para... This letter is to...

7. Nos es grato anunciarle que . . . We are pleased to announce that . . .

8. Me es grato recomendar a Ud. al Sr. . . . I take pleasure in recommending to you Mr. . . .

9. La presente tiene por objeto confirmarle nuestra conversación telefónica de esta mañana . . . This is to confirm our telephone conversation of this morning . . .

Ending a letter—

1. Anticipandole las gracias, saludo a Ud. atentamente,

   Thanking you in advance, we are
       Sincerely yours,

2. Anticipándoles las más expresivas gracias, quedamos de Uds.

       Attos. y SS.SS.

   Thanking you in advance, I am
       Sincerely yours,

3. Quedamos de Ud. atentos y Ss. Ss.

   We remain

       Sincerely yours,

4. En espera de sus gratas noticias, me repito de Ud.

       Atento y S.S.

   Hoping to hear from you, I am
       Sincerely yours,

5. Esperando su grata y pronta contestación, quedo,

       Su atento y S.S.

   Hoping to hear from you at your earliest convenience, I am

       Sincerely yours,

The following are often used when entering into a business correspondence:

6. Aprovecho esta ocasión para ofrecerme su atento y S.S.

Aprovechamos esta ocasión para suscribirnos,
Sus atentos y SS.SS

6. FORM OF THE ENVELOPE

Felix Valtueña y Cía
Calle de Zurbarán 6
Madrid

> Señor Don
> Ricardo Fitó,
> Apartado 5042,
> Barcelona

M. Navarro Suárez
San Martin 820
Buenos Aires

> Señores
> M. Suárez y Coello,
> Paseo de la Castellana 84,
> Madrid, España

Señorita
Vicenta Navarro,
63 Gran Vía de Germanías,
Valencia

Antonio de Suárez
Calle del Sol 2,
Chamartín de la Rosa,
Madrid

OTHER EXAMPLES

Sr. Don Antonio Aguilar[1]
Provenza, 95
Barcelona

Señorita
María Sucre y Navarro
Paseo de la Castellana, 80
Madrid

Señora Doña
Vicenta Navarro de Sucre
Gran Vía de Germanías, 63
Valencia

[1]To a doctor: Sr. Dr. Antonio Aguilar.
To an engineer: Sr. Ing. Don Antonio Aguilar.